Addressing the World

Addressing the World

National Identity and Internet Country Code Domains

Edited by Erica Schlesinger Wass

ROWMAN & LITTLEFIELD PUBLISHERS, INC.
Lanham • Boulder • New York • Toronto • Oxford

ROWMAN & LITTLEFIELD PUBLISHERS, INC.

Published in the United States of America
by Rowman & Littlefield Publishers, Inc.
A wholly owned subsidiary of the Rowman & Littlefield Publishing Group, Inc.
4501 Forbes Boulevard, Suite 200, Lanham, Maryland 20706
www.rowmanlittlefield.com

PO Box 317, Oxford OX2 9RU, United Kingdom

British Library Cataloguing in Publication Information Available

Library of Congress Cataloging-in-Publication Data

Addressing the world : national identity and Internet country code
domains / edited by Erica Schlesinger Wass.
       p. cm.
Includes bibliographical references and index.
ISBN: 978-0-7425-2810-9

   1. Internet domain names. I. Wass, Erica Schlesinger, 1976–
   TK5105.8835.A33 2003
   004.67'8—dc21

                                                          2003009131

Printed in the United States of America

♾™ The paper used in this publication meets the minimum requirements of
American National Standard for Information Sciences—Permanence of Paper for
Printed Library Materials, ANSI/NISO Z39.48-1992.

Contents

~

Acknowledgments

The idea for this book had been growing in my mind for several years before I first contacted a contributor. While the issues were gaining more prominence as time went on, I did not know whether anyone I contacted would be interested in joining me to explore the connections between cultures and domain names. My gratitude, therefore, lies heavily with my contributors: Dana M. Gallup, Tushar A. Gandhi, Toby E. Huff, Patrik Lindén, Martin Maguire, Paiki Muswazi, Patricio Poblete, Jenny Sinclair, Richard StClair, and Peter K. Yu, each of whom enthusiastically approached the project with creativity and a sense of purpose that encouraged me at every step. This book is a product not only of creativity but also of teamwork.

Despite our work, the book would likely not have been published without the support of acquisitions editor Brenda Hadenfeldt at Rowman & Littlefield. Always available to answer a question—or three—about both the content of the book and the publishing process, Brenda provided insight and encouragement throughout the process. Brenda, production editor Alden Perkins, and copyeditor Bruce Owens are the watchful eyes and thoughtful minds that are responsible for transforming this book from a virtual draft to a published manuscript. While all the writers had a sense of what they wanted to say, by no means did we work in a bubble. For their assistance and advice, we would like to thank Antony Van Couvering; the team at NIC Chile, especially their legal and business adviser, Margarita Valdez; Chai Choon Lee; Professor Zafar Ansari; John D. Harris; Amy

Gallup; the USC-ISI's Eric Mankin; USC's specialized libraries and archival collections archivist and manuscripts librarian Claude B. Zachary; Dr. Xue Hong; Cindy Zheng; Dr. Mao Wei; Dr. Hu Qiheng; Chris Disspain; Dr. Robert Elz; Glen Mulcaster; Dr. Andrew Herbert; Mark Hughes; Professor Peter Poole; Dr. Paul Twomey; and Mike van Niekerk.

On a personal note, I would like to thank all of my supportive family and friends, specifically, Tom Groppe, Shawn McIntosh, Michael Stockler, and Glen and Susan Weisman for their thoughtful conversations and editorial advice, the Wass family for their enthusiasm, and my parents, Helen and Stephen Schlesinger, who for years have encouraged me to pursue my dreams.

Last, thanks are not enough to give my husband, Troy. For the past two years, he has lived not only with me but also with this project. Throughout the initial brainstorming, the contacting of contributors and publishers, and the editing, he has supported me with both intelligence and compassion.

INTRODUCTION

~

Lots of Dots

Erica Schlesinger Wass

Conceived as a means of sharing research, the Internet has quickly become a medium that affects the way people learn, communicate, and even conduct business. The vast computer network appeals not only to skilled computer scientists but also to those without extensive technical ability. These days, in fact, most of the world is familiar with the structure of an Internet address; we have become accustomed to what are called Internet domain names, with the three Ws and the .com (read dot-com) that often sits at the end. There is much more to an Internet domain name than the generic .com, .org, and .net, however. In fact, there are more than 250 Internet address endings.[1]

Through the use of country code Internet domain name endings, the domain name system has gained the power to effect social change and incorporate national identities and priorities. It has, in the process, evolved into more than a technological convention; it is also a means of communicating cultural values.

Understanding the structure and content of Internet addresses can help people sift through the vast amount of online information and increase their understanding of people and places that are otherwise completely foreign. While the chapters in this book discuss culture and politics as much as if not more than pure technology, an early understanding of the Internet, its structure, and its history will illuminate many of the issues with respect to domain names.

When the Internet was developed, few knew how it would evolve. Yet, even at its earliest conception, the idea of using technology to effect social change was evident. The more psychologist Joseph Lickleder learned about computer science in the early 1960s, the more he believed that computers had the potential to transform society. He envisioned the day when home computer consoles and television sets would be linked in a massive network.[2] Today, such media convergence is on the verge of becoming a reality.

In October 1962, Lickleder was the first head of the U.S. government's computer research program at the Defense Advanced Research Projects Agency (DARPA, called ARPA at the time). He and scientist Robert Taylor envisioned a globally interconnected set of computers through which everyone could quickly access data and programs from any site.[3]

The goal, therefore, was to create a computer network that they called ARPANET; achieving that goal would require the help of many scientists, each working in a specialized field. Taylor hired Lawrence Roberts to lead the team that designed and developed ARPANET. Under Roberts's leadership, the team decided to use what was then an untested technology—packet switching—to send data between computers. Under the packet switching system, instead of using a dedicated connection between two computers, electronic messages are divided up into packets and transmitted over a decentralized network. Once all the packets arrive at the destination, they are recompiled into the original message. At the time, the technology was untested; its success is now confirmed whenever someone uses the Internet.

Under the guidance of even more computer scientists, ARPANET grew from four host computers in 1969 into what we now know as the Internet. Though the original technologies were successful at forming a network, developers soon sought a more advanced network that would better handle the enormous amount of traffic on the system. Responding to the need for more stability, Professors Robert Kahn and Vinton Cerf developed the Transmission Control Protocol (TCP), which was soon joined by the Internet Protocol (IP) to become the global standard for networked computer-to-computer communication.[4]

To understand the roles of TCP and IP, imagine that the information you want to send over a computer network is a puzzle—not a picture of a puzzle but a puzzle itself. TCP would be the protocol used to break the puzzle into individual pieces (the packets); IP would be used to send the pieces over the network, and TCP would then be responsible for locating any missing pieces and putting the puzzle back together again at the desired destination.

Under this system, IP acts as the mailman who delivers the packets. To ensure effective delivery, computers on the network are granted a numerical IP address. IP addresses are written as four numbers, each from 0 to 255, that are separated by periods, for example, 11.11.1.111. These addresses identify specific computers that operate across multiple networks.[5]

From the network's earliest days, the computers on the network were individually named so that they could be distinguished from one another. In 1973, the list that connected computer names to their IP addresses was stored on each computer in a file called hosts.txt.[6] As an increased number of computers was added to the network, however, this cataloging process became cumbersome and tedious because of both the sheer number of additions and the need to update changes locally. In addition, as more computers were added, the possibility for repeated names was increased; a large number of users wanted to name their computers Frodo, after Frodo Baggins, one of J. R. R. Tolkien's hobbits.[7]

Recognizing that there could not be more than one Frodo on the network and in response to the need for a more centralized naming system, in 1983 computer scientists and engineers Jonathan Postel, Paul Mockapetris, and Craig Partridge developed a new addressing scheme.

The Domain Name System (DNS) is novel in its organizational structure.[8] It is based on the hierarchical notion of tree branching. As Katie Hafner and Matthew Lyon wrote in *Where Wizards Stay Up Late*, "From the trunk to the branches, and outward to the leaves, every address would include levels of information representing, in progression, a smaller, more specific part of the network address."[9]

Though most Internet users read domain names from left to right, the underlying technology of the Internet reads them from right to left. As a result, the last part of the address that we read—.com, for example—is considered the top-level domain (TLD).

In 1983, .arpa was the first and only top-level domain created; all addresses on the network ended in .arpa.[10] Only a year later, Postel and his team had drawn the plan for the modern domain name system; they introduced .com, .edu, .gov, .mil, and .org and gave a rough layout for the addition of an additional set of two-letter codes that would identify countries.

In addition to his increasing domain name responsibilities, for many years Postel was also the editor of the Request for Comments (RFC) document series. First established in 1969, RFCs are memos written to introduce and discuss new ideas with other members of the technological community.[11] In RFC 920, Postel wrote, "While the initial domain name 'ARPA' arises from the history of the development of this system and environment, in the future most of the top level names will be very general categories like 'government,' 'education,' or 'commercial.'"[12] The motivation, he said, was to provide an organization name that was free of undesirable semantics.

By the mid-1980s, domain names were in widespread use.[13] The generic top-level domains (gTLDs), like .com, were in place, and the more than 240 two-lettered endings, like .uk and .jp, called country code top-level domains (ccTLDs), were implemented by Postel and were available for administrators to claim.[14]

When the domain names were developed, they were seen as a tool to enable the navigation of the network—to facilitate communication among the network's connected computers. They were not intended to communicate anything in themselves. In the past fifteen years, however, TLDs and ccTLDs, in particular, have, by their use and governance, constructed a space that outwardly communicates cultural identities and values.

When ccTLDs were developed, they were managed by volunteers and had no real value outside of academia. As the Internet became more commercial and governments saw a larger stake in their national codes, however, more attention was paid not only to the governance of the codes but also to what websites were allowed in their name spaces.

When Postel et al. first created the ccTLDs, they turned over management of the codes to friends and colleagues at universities and research foundations around the world. Early code delegations were made to the first person who requested one, provided that the administrative contact was located in the territory for which the code was named. As Professor Milton Mueller discusses in *Ruling the Root*, "Significantly, that delegation method tended to bypass completely the institutions in other countries that historically had possessed authority over communication, such as government ministries or posts, telephone, and telegraph monopolies."[15] While through the early 1990s few of these institutions paid close attention to the codes, as awareness of the Internet grew, so too did the codes' perceived value to many governments. In fact, arguments would soon erupt over whether national governments actually had ownership of the codes.

Mueller notes that when delegation conflicts began to occur more frequently, Postel subtly pushed the contenders to settle the disputes among themselves.[16] Once an administrator was selected, each manager was designated "the trustee of the top-level domain for both the nation, in the case of a country code, and the global Internet community."[17] Postel said that concerns about rights and ownership of domains were inappropriate, that managers and others should instead be concerned about responsibilities and service to the community. Several years later, he said, "That was written just as things were getting really commercial. There's been a very substantial change in the last three or four years, from a network that's primarily for academic use to a network that's overwhelmingly for commercial use. It's not appropriate for the academic world to subsidize the commercial world—maybe it should be the other way around. As the amount of commercial use has increased, it's become more appropriate to have these tasks be part of the economy. One must temper that, however, with what are practical commercial models. I still think the domain names are a kind of service."[18]

In 1989, Postel founded the Internet Assigned Numbers Authority (IANA). It was through the IANA, a U.S. government–funded body, that Postel controlled and monitored the allocation and assignment of Internet addresses. For many years, Postel not only worked at the IANA but was the IANA.[19] As the task grew in scope, however, he hired a small staff to aid in his work.

From the earliest conception of allocating national domain endings, Postel and his team could foresee endless discussion about what was or was not a nation and therefore what should or should not be included on the list of codes. They did not want to be arbiters of geopolitical debate. As a result, in RFC 1591, titled "Domain Name System Structure and Delegation," Postel wrote, "The IANA is not in the business of deciding what is and what is not a country." He did not want to become entrenched in the individual battles over which nations would receive ccTLD designations. He wanted to simplify the task of choosing which countries would get codes and what each code designation would be. To solve the problem, he turned to a preexisting list of codes that was provided and maintained by the International Organization for Standardization (ISO). [20]

In RFC 1591, Postel added, "The selection of the ISO 3166-1 list as a basis for country code top-level domain names was made with the knowledge that ISO has a procedure for determining which entities should be and should not be on that list."

Because it is the list that is the foundation for the actual two-letter codes, because it is the list that has the power to embolden a nation with a code, we must fully understand how nations are added to the list and how the interested parties have used the list to acquire national domain endings.

The ISO 3166-1 is used not only to designate ccTLDs but also to assess trade statistics in the European Union and to track FedEx shipments.[21] Many individuals, organizations, and unrecognized political entities interested in obtaining their own ccTLDs have requested to be included in the ISO 3166-1 list. "Such requests are absolutely futile," the ISO says. There are strict procedures for adding a code to the list.[22]

The only way to enter a new country name into ISO 3166-1 is to have it registered in either the United Nations Terminology Bulletin "Country Names" or the United Nations Statistics Division's "Country and Region Codes for Statistical Use." Those listed in "Country Names" are either a UN member country, a member of one of its specialized agencies, or a party to the Statute of the International Court of Justice. Once a country name or territory name appears in either of these two sources, it is added to the ISO 3166-1 automatically.

As per RFC 1591, Postel requires a nation to be on the ISO 3166-1 list to become a ccTLD, and despite a few exceptions, which have also been called mistakes, the list of ccTLDs mirrors the ISO 3166-1. One of the most obvious exceptions is that the code for the United Kingdom on the ISO 3166-1 list is .gb, while the ccTLD for the United Kingdom is .uk.[23] There are several theories for the discrepancy.

In RFC 3071, titled "Reflections on the DNS, RFC 1591, and Categories of Domains," John C. Klensin noted that the adoption of .uk was historical in nature.[24] The notion is that .uk was chosen as a logical code for the United Kingdom before the policy of using the ISO list was settled. Others suggest it was merely a mistake.

As domain administrator Martin Maguire discusses in chapter 2, as ccTLDs have gained more economic and political value, the naming system has come under increased scrutiny. While special rules are being passed for some domains, a thorough examination of the list shows that other known political or geographic entities are not included. For example, many now argue that Scotland, Northern Ireland, England, and Wales should have their own ccTLDs as opposed to being grouped under the larger .uk.[25]

By the late 1980s, while both the gTLD and ccTLD systems were in place and there were many computers linked to the network, there was no easy way to navigate the vast information they stored. In 1990, Tim Berners-Lee, a software engineer at the European Particle Physics Laboratory CERN, developed an easier way for researchers to access the vast amount of research documents on the Internet. He named his project the "World Wide Web" because he visualized it as a web of interconnected documents that would stretch across the Internet and the world.[26]

Berners-Lee's team at CERN, in collaboration with the National Center for Supercomputing Applications (NCSA), a federally funded research facility at the University of Illinois at Urbana-Champaign, produced the first version of the Hypertext Markup Language (HTML), the coding language used to create documents for use on the World Wide Web. An entirely text-based system, the early web would probably be unrecognizable to most modern Internet users. While there was an enormous potential for reading and typing, there was no clicking, passive watching, or listening. The web's origins are reminiscent of a newspaper. Berners-Lee sought to allow access to black-and-white readable information. The web's next innovators wanted to emulate a different mass media model—television.

Marc Andreessen, an undergraduate computer science major at the University of Illinois, wanted to put a more "human face" on Berners-Lee's web.[27] Working at NCSA, he and some friends developed the first popular graphical web browser, NCSA Mosaic; he would later develop the Netscape line of web browser. By allowing the use of color, images, sounds, video, and a mouse to navigate, the web quickly moved away from its text-based roots and came to resemble television more than a newspaper.

With the prospects of communication and commerce, the simple navigation of web links drew large numbers of people online. The shift in use of the Internet also signaled a shift in Internet governance.

Under the leadership of Postel and IANA, through the mid-1990s, DNS functions were based in a noncompetitive, government-funded system. In 1996, Postel initiated an Internet ad hoc committee to institutionalize the IANA functions and open top-level domains to competitive registration. The U.S. Department of Commerce responded to Postel's call and published a white paper that envisioned a "global, consensus, non-profit corporation" to govern the Internet naming system.[28]

In October 1998, just before Postel died from complications following cardiac surgery at age fifty-five, he went so far as to propose bylaws for the entity that would take over the responsibility for administering policy for the Internet address system. Within weeks, the Internet Corporation for Assigned Names and Numbers (ICANN), a nonprofit California-based corporation, assumed the functions of IANA as part of the transfer of Internet administration to the private sector. ICANN has been steeped in controversy ever since.[29]

Called the Internet's own Obi-Wan Kenobi, "the sage who guided the Net from its sleepy academic genesis to its present form," by *Wired News*, Postel displayed a hippie sensibility.[30] He was not interested in making money or in politics; he was a "techie."[31]

Postel saw the codes as merely an online equivalent to postal codes. Instead, just as American television's best-known ZIP code "90210" became synonymous with the rich Beverly Hills lifestyle, country code domain names began to take on more political and social meaning. As Martin Maguire discusses in chapter 2, East Timor's .tp was used as a platform from which to launch political protest and help bring freedom to a colonized people.

The local struggles are mirrored in the global system. Many controversies have erupted among ccTLD registrars and managers as well as in the larger Internet community, in part because of the sheer number of ccTLDs with diverse rules and the ever-evolving interest in the domain names. In chapter 1, law professor Peter K. Yu discusses the origins and development of ccTLD lawmaking. These controversies were hardly envisioned when the system was created.

In Chile, India, and Malaysia the local cultures have directly affected the use and development of the ccTLDs. In chapter 3, Patricio Poblete, who administers Chile's .cl, discusses why the Chilean people have rallied around the use of .cl to such a level that it has become the most popular top-level domain in Chile. The result of this high use is that the Chilean culture is not dispersed on the Internet among many TLDs but is concentrated in .cl. In contrast, despite a population of one billion, there is little use of India's .in.

In chapter 4, Tushar A. Gandhi, an Internet developer and great-grandson of Mahatma Gandhi, explains why Indians have virtually no national identity on the web and how he is working to change that.

In chapter 5, sociology and anthropology professor Toby E. Huff presents the results of his original research on domain identification among Malaysian students. Huff, a noted scholar on the Islamic world, discovers that among Malaysian students there is a strong desire not to be seen as provincial. That yearning, in addition to strict .my registration policies and privacy and surveillance concerns, may incline young Malaysians to opt for international identities.

The book then examines the relationship between national priorities and the ways ccTLDs are used to achieve them. As discussed earlier, each ccTLD administrator has the right to establish guidelines that correspond with the nation's cultural and political norms. This is evident in the stories of Sweden's .se and Niue's .nu. In chapter 6, Patrik Lindén, a communications officer at the organization responsible for managing Sweden's .se, discusses how Sweden established strict guidelines for those who wanted to register domains under .se. Some TLDs, like .com, can be quickly registered, with no prior assessment of whether the registrant has a legitimate use for that address; other TLDs, like .se, chose a prior assessment model, making the initial registration more difficult. As a result of the regulations, many Swedes stopped registering .se domains. In fact, sites ending in gTLD .com and ccTLD .nu accounted for almost half the nearly 126,000 Swedish websites found in 2001. Seeking to draw Swedes back to .se and reestablish a national identity online, more liberalized regulations were implemented in April 2003.

But Sweden's loss has been Niue's gain. Niue (pronounced "new-way") is the beneficiary of .nu, one of the first ccTLDs to be marketed to those outside its host nation. In chapter 7, Richard StClair, the technical manager for .nu, discusses how in many ways .nu is successful because of .se's cautious policies. As Swedish people fled .se, many registered their sites under .nu (which means "now" in Swedish). The resources generated by those sales are used to develop and maintain the Internet services on Niue; excess funding is dispersed through a local advisory board into other fields, such as health, education, and community services. The result of the high number of registrations is the ability to provide entirely free Internet access for each of the South Pacific island's 1,500 permanent residents.

Of course, Niue is not the only ccTLD to market a catchy code to the world. Tuvalu's .tv, Micronesia and Armenia's .fm and .am, and Moldova's .md are among those codes marketed to the global population. In chapter 8, attorney Dana M. Gallup shares his personal experiences with the licensing and marketing of .md.

It is not only small nations that allow outsiders to register domains within their local ccTLD name spaces. In October 2002, China eased the registration rules for its ccTLD .cn; it has relaxed its highly restrictive registration policy and now not only allows but also encourages foreign business to register .cn domain names. In chapter 9, I discuss how China has developed ccTLD policies that reflect the nation's larger attempts to open its doors and integrate its economy with Western nations.

Conversely, in chapter 10, librarian Paiki Muswazi introduces Swaziland's .sz as an example of a developing nation that markets its ccTLD not to the outside world but to its own people. The use of .sz can be divided into broad categories, namely, e-commerce, communication, cultural promotion, and social and political regulation. Both emerging technologies and the lure of tourism revenue have the potential to deepen the indigenous essence of .sz and to consolidate its cultural content.

Though seen as virtually dormant since its creation, a recent restructuring of the .us name space has provided a more patriotic domain opportunity for those having significant contacts with the United States. In chapter 11, I introduce .us, which for years had been underutilized both because of extreme indecision over its structure and purpose and because of the popularity and accessibility of .com. In the fall of 2001, however, the control of .us was awarded to a Washington-based firm, and the marketing of American online patriotism has been a staple ever since.

The passing of the torch from one ccTLD manager to another is called redelegation. In many ways, it represents the end of an era in ccTLD management. While Postel granted trusteeship of the ccTLDs to his colleagues, who for years volunteered their time to management of the domains, as both popular and governmental interest in ccTLDs grew, the task became too large for these individuals. Postel's designated administrators now often bow out or, as in the case of Australia's .au, feel pushed out of their longtime positions. In chapter 12, journalist Jenny Sinclair introduces us to .au and its outspoken, now former manager, Robert Elz, who devoted his time and energy to fulfilling Postel's vision and found himself in the middle of one of the most contentious redelegations to date.

Country code domains, once seen merely as street signs for computer networks, are now indicators of national cultures, identities, and priorities. Each code—and each contributor in this book—has a perspective to share and a story to tell; I hope you enjoy them all.

Notes

1. See this book's appendix.

2. Katie Hafner and Matthew Lyon, *Where Wizards Stay Up Late: The Origins of the Internet* (New York: Touchstone, 1996), 34.

3. "A Brief History of the Internet," ISOC www.isoc.org/internet/history/brief.shtml#Introduction [accessed March 13, 2003].

4. Robert X. Cringely, "NERDS 2.01: Networking the Nerds," PBS, 1998, www.pbs.org/opb/nerds2.0.1/networking_nerds/tcpip.html [accessed March 13, 2003].

5. To find out your IP address, see www.ed-phys.fr/htbin/ipaddress [accessed March 13, 2003]; to convert an IP address to a host name and vice versa, see cello.cs.uiuc.edu/cgi-bin/slamm/ip2name [accessed March 13, 2003].

6. L. Peter Deutsch, "Host Names On-line" (Network Working Group, Request for Comments No. 606), December 1973, www.rfc-editor.org/rfc/rfc606.txt [accessed March 13, 2003].

7. Haffner and Lyon, *Wizards*, 252.

8. P. Mockapetris, "Domain Names—Concepts and Facilities" (Network Working Group, Request for Comments No. 882), November 1983, www.rfc-editor.org/rfc/rfc882.txt [accessed March 13, 2003].

9. Haffner and Lyon, *Wizards*, 253.

10. J. Postel, "The Domain Names Plan and Schedule" (Network Working Group, Request for Comments No. 881), November 1983, www.rfc-editor.org/rfc/rfc881.txt [accessed March 13, 2003].

11. For more on RFCs, see "30 Years of RFCs" (Network Working Group, Request for Comments No. 2555), April 7, 1999, www.rfc-editor.org/rfc/rfc2555.txt [accessed March 13, 2003].

12. J. Postel and J. Reynolds "Domain Requirements" (Network Working Group, Request for Comments No. 920), October 1984, www.rfc-editor.org/rfc/rfc920.txt [accessed March 13, 2003].

13. Jon Postel, "Testimony to the U.S. House of Representatives Committee on Science Subcommittee on Basic Research," September 25, 1997, www.house.gov/science/postel_9-25.html [accessed September 13, 2002].

14. In 1985, three ccTLDs were delegated; see "History of the Internet: ccTLDs in Chronological Order of Top Level Domain Creation at the Internic," www.wwtld.org/aboutcctld/history/wwtld1999/ccTLDs-by-date.html [accessed March 13, 2003].

15. Milton L. Mueller, *Ruling the Root: Internet Governance and the Taming of Cyberspace* (Cambridge, Mass.: MIT Press, 2002), 88.

16. Mueller, *Ruling the Root*, 89.

17. Jon Postel, "Domain Name System Structure and Delegation" (Network Working Group, Request for Comments No. 1591), March 1994, www.rfc-editor.org/rfc/rfc1591.txt [accessed March 13, 2003].

18. Diane Krieger, "An Interview with Jon Postel," *NetWorker* 7, no. 5 (Summer 1997): 2, www.usc.edu/isd/publications/networker/96-97/Summer_97/innerview-postel2.html [accessed March 13, 2003].

19. See, for example, Vint Cerf, "I Remember IANA" (Network Working Group, Request for Comments No. 2468), October 1998, www.rfc-editor.org/rfc/rfc2468.txt [accessed March 13, 2003].

20. "ISO" is not an acronym; the name "ISO" is a word, derived from the Greek "isos," meaning "equal"; see "What Is ISO?" International Organization for Standardization, www.iso.ch/iso/en/aboutiso/introduction/whatisISO.html [accessed March 13, 2003].

21. See "The Implementation of ISO 3166-1," International Organization for Standardization, www.iso.ch/iso/en/prods-services/iso3166ma/04background-on-iso-3166/implementations-of-iso3166-1.html [accessed September 13, 2002]. Of note, the ISO is located in Switzerland; its ccTLD is .ch, the code for Switzerland. (Because Switzerland has four national languages, each of which spells the nation differently, Swiss coins, license plates, and domain names refer to the Latin name "Confoederatio Helvetica" [Swiss Confederation], hence .ch.)

22. "ISO 3166-1 and Country Coded Top-Level Domains (ccTLDs)," International Organization for Standardization, www.iso.ch/iso/en/prods-services/iso3166ma/04background-on-iso-3166/iso3166-1-and-ccTLDs.html [accessed September 13, 2002].

23. For a discussion of the history and development of .uk, see Daniel J. Paré, *Internet Governance in Transition: Who Is the Master of This Domain?* (New York: Rowman & Littlefield, 2003).

24. John C. Klensin, "RFC 3071: Reflections on the DNS, RFC 1591, and Categories of Domains" (Network Working Group, Request for Comments No. 3071), February 2001, www.rfc-editor.org/rfc/rfc3071.txt [accessed March 13, 2003].

25. "Scotland Entering New Domain," BBC News, May 1, 2000, news.bbc.co.uk/1/hi/scotland/732199.stm [accessed March 13, 2003].

26. See Tim Berners-Lee, *Weaving the Web: The Original Design and Ultimate Destiny of the World Wide Web* (New York: HarperBusiness, 2000).

27. Robert X. Cringely, "NERDS 2.01: A Human Face," PBS, 1998, www.pbs.org/opb/nerds2.0.1/wiring_world/mosaic.html [accessed March 13, 2003].

28. U.S. Department of Commerce, "Statement of Policy," June 5, 1998, www.icann.org/general/white-paper-05jun98.htm [accessed March 13, 2003].

29. See, for example, discussions at ICANNWatch at www.icannwatch.org [accessed March 13, 2003].

30. "New Internet Government Forged," *WiredNews*, September 17, 1998, www.wired.com/news/politics/0,1283,14795,00.html [accessed March 13, 2003].

31. "Esther Dyson on the Internet, ICANN and Doing Business Abroad," Knowledge@Wharton, April 10, 2002, knowledge.wharton.upenn.edu/articles.cfm?catid=9&articleid=542 [accessed March 13, 2003].

~

CHAPTER ONE

The Never-Ending ccTLD Story

Peter K. Yu

Adding to their complexity, country code top-level domains (ccTLDs) are governed at both the micro and the macro level. While local ccTLD managers have, for example, the authority to determine the requirements to register a domain name, larger governing bodies set out to coordinate policy among the 240 codes.

Michigan State University law professor Peter K. Yu demystifies the history of ccTLD policymaking. He explains that ccTLD lawmaking has transitioned from ad hoc decision making to institutional and self-interested wrangling. What will emerge will be a system of international lawmaking that will take national norms into consideration.

A long time ago in a galaxy not so far away, there was a decentralized, global network of computers. These computers shared information with each other regardless of how far apart they were and whether there was any direct line of communication. In the very beginning, this network was used exclusively by government and military agencies, educational and research institutions, government contractors, scientists, and technological specialists.[1] Instead of the domain names we use today, such as "www.amazon.com," users typed in numeric addresses, such as "123.45.67.89," and later host names to send information to other computers.[2]

This network soon expanded, and domain names became a practical necessity for two reasons.[3] First, alphabetical texts are generally easier for humans to remember than numeric addresses. Second, as Internet traffic increases and as computer systems get reconfigured, the computer server that is used for a particular website may change from time to time. In fact, some busy websites might use multiple servers, requiring them to take turns to address requests directed to a single domain name. While the website owner (or his or her technical staff) might know internally which numeric address the website corresponds to at a particular moment, the general public does not. Domain names are therefore needed for identification purposes.

Although domain names are easy for humans to remember, computers do not understand these catchy names. Instead, they have to "translate" these names back to numeric addresses before they can locate the information the users requested. To maximize efficiency and minimize storage, the Domain Name System (DNS) was designed as a hierarchy, like a pyramid. To "resolve" a domain name, the computer issues a query to the name server at the bottom of the hierarchy. If the computer fails to obtain an answer, it will move up the hierarchy. If it still does not obtain an answer, it will continue to move up the hierarchy until it finally succeeds.

At the apex of this hierarchy is a set of thirteen root zone servers that identify the name servers storing the root zone files for all the top-level domains, including both the generic domains—such as .com, .net, or .org—and country code top-level domains (ccTLDs).[4] Each of these servers is assigned a letter from A to M. For example, the Internet Software Consortium operates the "F Root Server," and the server in London is called the "K Root Server." More than three-quarters of these servers are located in the United States, and the rest are found in Japan, Sweden, and the United Kingdom.

To perform its identifying function, a domain name needs to be unique. Thus, all root zone files must contain identical data.[5] As a past legacy, the database in the A Root Server, which the Internet Corporation for Assigned Names and Numbers (ICANN) currently controls by virtue of its contract with the U.S. Department of Commerce (DoC), is considered authoritative. The other root servers merely copy this root zone file to their servers.

Because of this hierarchy and the lucrative market created by the sale of domain names, there has been an ongoing power struggle over the control of the DNS and authority to delegate and administer ccTLDs. This chapter recounts the story of this struggle. It traces how ccTLD policymaking has been transformed from ad hoc, informal coordination to international, contract-based governance. It also discusses the various major players in the ccTLD debate: ICANN, the Internet Assigned Numbers Authority (IANA), ccTLD managers, national governments, the International Telecommunication Union (ITU), and the World Intellectual Property Organization (WIPO).

This story began when scientists, including Jon Postel and Paul Mock-apetris, developed the DNS in 1983.[6] Under a contract with the U.S. government, Postel and later IANA managed the DNS and delegated ccTLDs to foreign managers.[7] The first ccTLD, .us, was created and delegated in March 1985 (see chapter 11).[8] Two other delegations, .uk (for the United Kingdom) and .il (for Israel), followed in the same year.

In the very beginning, many countries were not connected to the Internet backbone and, therefore, had no need for a ccTLD. Even when they needed one, ccTLD delegations usually fell into the hands of university computer science departments and educational and research networking organizations rather than government agencies and organizations that historically provided postal, telephone, or telegraph services.[9]

From 1985 to 1993, Postel delegated ccTLDs on a first-come, first-served basis. Using the notion of a "responsible person," Postel required very limited basic administrative criteria before he delegated a ccTLD. As he wrote, the person in charge of assigning second-level domain names "is generally the first person that asks for the job (and is somehow considered a 'responsible person')."[10]

To avoid political problems, Postel used the ISO 3166-1 country codes to define what entity would warrant a ccTLD.[11] Because these codes were provided by the International Organization for Standardization (ISO), an international association of national standard-setting bodies, their objectivity successfully shielded IANA from the political pressure of deciding what was and what was not a country.

Although the use of ISO 3166-1 codes appears systematic and well planned, the .uk ccTLD betrayed the ad hoc nature of early ccTLD policy-making.[12] The ISO 3166-1 country code for the United Kingdom is .gb (for "Great Britain"). Yet, Postel assigned .uk as the country's ccTLD. Moreover, during a brief period in 1996, IANA delegated codes under the ISO 3166 reserve list, which the ISO 3166 Maintenance Agency reserved specifically for postal purposes.[13]

Notwithstanding the ad hoc nature of ccTLD delegation, conflicts rarely arose. Even if they did, when two parties competed for the same ccTLD, Postel usually succeeded in using subtle pressure to induce disputing parties to settle the issue before delegation.[14] As IANA reasoned in a later document, dispute resolution "is usually a long drawn out process, leaving at least one party unhappy, so it is far better when the parties can reach an agreement among themselves."[15]

By the early 1990s, the Internet had exploded onto the world stage. As more countries became connected and as national governments (and private companies) began to realize the full socioeconomic potential of a ccTLD, requests for ccTLD delegations increased substantially. The number of ccTLD delegations went from 46 in 1990 to 108 in 1993. By the mid-1990s, IANA had delegated virtually all the ccTLDs, including those in countries that had limited Internet access.[16]

With the increasing interest in ccTLDs, a more explicit delegation and administration policy was in order. In March 1994, Postel published RFC 1591, which described his delegation and administration policy.[17] It stated, first and foremost, that there must be a designated manager for supervising the ccTLD name space and that the administrative contact must reside in the country. Because the manager is the "trustee" for both the nation and the global Internet community, the manager must be equitable to all those who request domain names. In addition, the manager must do a "satisfactory job" of operating the DNS service for the domain, and "significantly interested parties" in the domain must agree that the delegation is appropriate.

Moreover, RFC 1591 ensured that IANA would strictly adhere to the ISO 3166-1 list as the basis of ccTLD delegations. As the document stated, "IANA is not in the business of deciding what is and what is not a country." Should a dispute arise, IANA would "try to have any contending parties reach agreement among themselves, and generally take no action to change things unless all the contending parties agree." IANA would intervene only "in cases where the designated manager has substantially misbehaved," although RFC 1591 did not indicate what constituted misbehavior.

Since the publication of RFC 1591, IANA has issued a number of ccTLD News Memos.[18] Although many of these memos were issued for communication purposes, the first memo addressed the relationship between ccTLD managers and national governments. It stated that IANA "takes the desires of the government of the country very seriously, and will take them as a major consideration in any transition discussion."[19]

Notwithstanding RFC 1591 and the first ccTLD News Memo, controversies existed. For example, RFC 1591 required that ccTLD managers reside in the requested domain. Yet, a British company successfully registered Libya's ccTLD, .ly, by listing its owner's Tripoli address as the address of the administrative contact.[20] In addition, IANA has delegated ccTLDs to unaccountable commercial entities that had limited ties to the concerned domain. Out of recourse from IANA, the government of Bhutan sought assistance from the ITU, the UN-affiliated body that governs international telecommunications matters, to reclaim its ccTLD, .bt.[21] Even worse, IANA was dragged into domestic disputes and had to make arbitrary decisions in the case concerning Haiti's ccTLD, .ht.[22]

Moreover, not all political entities were included in the ISO 3166-1 list, and those omitted were understandably concerned about how IANA's actions (or the lack thereof) could frustrate their political aspirations. For example, the Palestinians did not receive the .ps domain until the ISO 3166-1 list included the Occupied Palestinian Territory.[23] Conversely, despite its dissolution in 1991, the Soviet Union continues to exist in cyberspace because IANA fails to delete the .su domain from the root zone file.[24]

The European Union is equally unhappy about the ISO 3166-1 codes. Despite its size and economic importance, it failed to obtain its .eu name space because the ISO 3166-1 list does not recognize supranational entities.[25] In September 2000, the ICANN board finally passed a resolution approving the delegation of the .eu ccTLD.[26] The European Commission subsequently adopted the regulation for the creation of the yet-to-be-determined .eu registry.[27]

Meanwhile, the Internet had become increasingly commercial and global. By the mid-1990s, the U.S. government decided to privatize the DNS.[28] Following a request for comments from the public, the DoC published a proposal to reform the DNS administration in January 1998.[29] Known as the DNS Green Paper, this proposal mapped out the Clinton administration's domain name policy and explained why the DoC had authority to regulate the DNS. Although the Green Paper was intended to be consultative by nature, many found the document controversial.

In light of this reaction, the DoC abandoned its original rule-making plan. Instead, it issued a nonbinding statement of policy that became known as the DNS White Paper.[30] The White Paper delineated four basic principles that were used to develop the new DNS system, namely, "stability, competition, private bottom-up coordination, and representation." Noting the need to withdraw the U.S. government from DNS administration, the policy statement called for the establishment of a private entity that would take over the DNS. As the White Paper stated, "Overall policy guidance and control of the TLDs [top-level domains] and the Internet root server system should be vested in a single organization that is representative of Internet users around the globe."

In addition, the White Paper noted that "neither national governments acting as sovereigns nor intergovernmental organizations acting as representatives of governments should participate in management of Internet names and addresses." Nonetheless, the White Paper recognized the need to ensure international input into the new DNS. It also acknowledged the authority of national governments "to manage or establish policy for their own ccTLDs."

Finally, the White Paper identified cybersquatting—the preemptive registration of trademarks as domain names by third parties—as a major problem in the DNS. It called on WIPO to "initiate a balanced and transparent process" to provide the new entity with recommendations on how to deal with cybersquatting. Pursuant to this invitation, WIPO launched the First WIPO Internet Domain Name Process, a lengthy and extensive global consultative process that involved consultation meetings in fourteen countries in six continents and the participation of a large number of government agencies, intergovernmental organizations, professional associations, corporations, and individuals.[31]

Shortly after the DoC published the White Paper, ICANN was incorporated as a private not-for-profit corporation in California, with Postel as its chief technical officer and a board of directors who had limited knowledge of the Internet and domain name matters.[32] In November 1998, the DoC entered into an agreement with ICANN concerning the transfer of DNS management.[33] To take over IANA's operation, ICANN also entered into an agreement with the Information Sciences Institute at the University of Southern California, where Postel worked until his untimely death.[34]

A few months later, the DoC officially recognized ICANN as the private entity mentioned in the White Paper.[35] As Professor Michael Froomkin observed, this development was "no coincidence: The whole point of the White Paper had been to find a more formal structure for DNS management that left it in Postel's capable hands—and could be presented as a pro-Internet, deregulatory victory for the Clinton administration (and Ira Magaziner). ICANN exists because the Department of Commerce called for it to exist."[36]

Structurally, ICANN benefits from the input of its directors, supporting organizations, and special advisory committees.[37] The committee that deals with global policy and ccTLD matters is the Governmental Advisory Committee (GAC), which is regularly attended by national governments, distinct economies, and intergovernmental organizations, such as the ITU and WIPO. Under the recently reformed structure, the GAC provides direct advice to the ICANN board and appoints liaisons to the board, the committee that nominates the directors, and the various supporting organizations.[38]

To "announce" its taking over IANA's function and to emphasize its authority over ccTLD matters, ICANN issued ICP-1 (ICANN Corporate Policy) in May 1999.[39] Combining RFC 1591 and the ccTLD News Memo #1, this document strengthened the power of national governments on ccTLD matters. As it stated, "The desires of the government of a country with regard to delegation of a ccTLD are taken very seriously. The IANA will make them a major consideration in any TLD delegation/transfer discussions."

In February 2000, the GAC presented to ICANN the "Principles for Delegation and Administration of ccTLDs" (GAC Principles),[40] which ICANN later used extensively to justify its redelegation efforts. Although the GAC Principles sought to provide "the model for institutionalizing the relationship between ICANN, ccTLD delegations, and the relevant national governments or public authorities,"[41] many found the document controversial and antithetical to the interests of ccTLD managers.

Since its establishment, ICANN has delegated the .ps to the Occupied Palestinian Territory and deleted Zaire's .zr in light of the country's change of name.[42] It has also redelegated ten ccTLDs—Pitcairn Island's .pn, Canada's .ca, Australia's .au (see chapter 12), Japan's .jp, Burundi's .bi, Malawi's .mw, Laos's .la, Sudan's .sd, Kenya's .ke, and Afghanistan's .af.[43] ICANN has entered into contractual relationships with all the new ccTLD managers upon redelegation, with the exception of Canada's.[44]

In addition, ICANN has been working actively with other ccTLD managers to document their relationships, which vary greatly with respect to the type of organization, policies followed, economics, language, culture, legal environment, and relations with governments.[45] While ICANN expected ccTLD managers to enter into contracts in which the managers would acknowledge ICANN's authority and would agree to contribute fees to the organization,[46] the managers refused. In response, the managers questioned ICANN's authority and criticized the organization for its lack of openness, accountability, and representation.

In February 2002, ICANN President Stuart Lynn openly admitted the need for reforms, something critics have advocated since ICANN's establishment.[47] He wrote, "If ICANN comes to be seen . . . as simply a tool of the U.S. Government, it will no longer have any hope of accomplishing its original mission." Seeking to reconcile the organization's relationship with ccTLD managers, the proposal recommended that ICANN replace the five at-large board seats with government representatives.

In December 2002, ICANN finally completed its reforms.[48] Under the new structure, ICANN has a volunteer board of directors, including fifteen voting and six nonvoting members, all of whom will be selected by the supporting organizations and ICANN's Nominating Committee. To facilitate interests of the ccTLD managers and national governments, a new Country-Code Name Supporting Organization (ccNSO) will be established.

While ICANN remains relevant to the ccTLD debate, the increasing concern of ccTLD managers and national governments over ccTLD policy-making might affect how ICANN develops its policy. As Kenneth Cukier pointed out, ccTLD managers have the potential to control ICANN's future: "The confederation of independent ccTLD administrators could bring ICANN vitally-needed legitimacy and funding if it formally recognizes the authority of ICANN and pay it fees. Conversely, if the ccTLD community continues to balk from establishing a formal relationship with ICANN, it would weaken the institution."[49] After all, if the ccTLD managers could convince the DoC that ICANN could not handle ccTLD matters, the DoC might decide not to renew ICANN's contract.

Apart from ccTLD managers, national governments have played an increasingly important role in the ccTLD debate. In a recent survey, Professor Michael Geist found a diverse array of relationships between national governments and ccTLD managers.[50] While government agencies and departments manage ten ccTLDs, national governments have contractual or informal relationships with many others. Some registries, like those in Canada and the United States, also create a relationship between the country and the domain name registrants by requiring local presence as a prerequisite to registration.[51]

Today, national governments recognize ccTLDs "as a component of their sovereignty and a vital national interest."[52] Realizing that ccTLDs may denote the "brand of the country," some governments openly embrace ccTLDs as "a platform for national economic growth and the institutions of civil society brought online."[53] Some, like Tuvalu, even use ccTLDs as a revenue-generating source, selling off rights in their name spaces for tens of millions of dollars.[54]

As ccTLDs become increasingly important, national governments have begun to assert control over the administration of their ccTLDs. For example, Australia, Canada, and Japan have petitioned ICANN for the redelegation of their domains. Likewise, the European Union is working closely with ICANN to create the .eu name space.

However, not all governments are interested in working with ICANN. Some might prefer to act alone or to abandon ICANN for a more favorable international forum, such as the ITU.[55] Indeed, some governments have already sought to use national legislation to regulate local ccTLD managers. A case in point is the government of South Africa, which recently introduced legislation to reclaim control of the .za name space from the incumbent ccTLD manager.[56] Similarly, during the controversial redelegation of the .au domain, the Australian government reminded ICANN that "as a last resort the Australian Government could invoke legislation relating to the self-regulation of the domain name system."[57]

Legally, some governments can consider using the "eminent domain" doctrine,[58] which, if applicable, allows governments to take away private property at fair market value to promote an overriding public interest.[59] Given the socioeconomic importance of a ccTLD, these governments would likely be able to convince the courts that their actions are constitutional. Nonetheless, such governmental action might not be desirable, for it would bring formal political control over the ccTLD system and impose constraints on the DNS that ICANN was designed to prevent.[60]

To break free of ICANN, the governments could also join together to establish an alternative root zone file or a system of root zone files that replaces the current root zone file. ICANN's governance structure is premised on the general consensus that there can be only one authoritative root zone file, lest there be inefficiency, inconnectivity, economic injury, or even chaos in the DNS. However, if governments become so frustrated with ICANN that they would rather risk infrastructure damages than remain subjected to an overbearing "Leviathan," many might consider alternative roots desirable.[61]

Finally, in the absence of ICANN's intervention or oversight, the international community could work together to develop a "code of practice" to promote harmonization and compliance while minimizing disputes. For example, they could draft an international treaty that sets the parameters of ccTLD management and administration practice. They could also work together to develop a nonbonding document that provides guiding principles to ccTLD managers and national governments.

A case in point is the *WIPO ccTLD Best Practices for the Prevention and Resolution of Property Disputes*,[62] which WIPO released in June 2001. This document provides voluntary guidelines concerning registration practices and dispute resolution procedures. These guidelines were particularly needed because ccTLD managers retain the power to set policies for their domain—for example, they can decide whether registrants have to be residents of the country, whether they are subject to the Uniform Dispute Resolution Policy (UDRP), and whether their personal information will be displayed on a publicly available WHOIS database, which, traditionally, allows anyone to look up individual domain names and view the registrant's contact and network information.

Of notable interest is the final section of the report, which advocates the adoption of the UDRP in the absence of any contrary local privacy regulations.[63] The UDRP was introduced in October 1999. It sets forth the terms and conditions related to a dispute between the registrant and a third party over the registration and use of a domain name.[64] Although commentators have criticized the UDRP for its procedural weaknesses,[65] the policy has been widely acclaimed for its simplicity and cost-effectiveness in resolving trademark disputes. Since the UDRP entered into force in December 1999, thousands of cases have been filed, and the majority of these cases has been resolved satisfactorily and efficiently.

Over the next few years, the struggle for control of the DNS and ccTLD delegations will likely continue. Unlike this story, however, the sequel will be very different. There is little doubt that the story will still include ICANN, IANA, ccTLD managers, national governments, GAC, ITU, and WIPO. However, the story will also feature new, emerging players, like ccNSO, CENTR (Council of European National Top-Level Domain Registries),[66] powerful individual ccTLD managers,[67] intellectual property rights holders, Internet Service Providers, and major telecommunications and information technology companies. As a result, few can forecast how the future will unfold.

Notes

I would like to thank Kenneth Cukier, Tamar Frankel, Michael Geist, Milton Mueller, and Jonathan Weinberg for their helpful comments and suggestions on earlier drafts of this chapter.

1. For interesting discussion of the origin of the Internet, see generally Tim Berners-Lee, *Weaving the Web: The Original Design and Ultimate Destiny of the World Wide Web* (New York: HarperBusiness, 2000); Katie Hafner and Matthew Lyon, *Where Wizards Stay Up Late: The Origins of the Internet* (New York: Touchstone, 1996); John Naughton, *A Brief History of the Future: From Radio Days to Internet Years in a Lifetime* (New York: Overlook Press, 2000); and Barry M. Leiner et al., "A Brief History of the Internet," August 4, 2000, www.isoc.org/internet/history/brief.shtml [accessed March 20, 2003].

2. The use of host names dates back to 1974. See M. D. Kudlick, "Host Names On-Line" (Network Working Group, Request for Comments No. 608), January 10, 1974, www.rfc-editor.org/rfc/rfc608.txt [accessed March 20, 2003]. By 1977, the use of numeric addresses was "strongly discouraged"; see David H. Crocker et al., "Standard for the Format of Arpa Network Text Messages (1)" (Network Working Group, Request for Comments No. 733), November 21, 1977, 19, www.rfc-editor.org/rfc/rfc733.txt [accessed March 20, 2003]. See also Jonathan Weinberg, "ICANN and the Problem of Legitimacy," *Duke Law Journal* 50, no. 1 (October 2000): 187–260, 194–95 (discussing pre-DNS Internet addressing).

3. See Milton L. Mueller, *Ruling the Root: Internet Governance and the Taming of Cyberspace* (Cambridge, Mass.: MIT Press, 2002), 39–40.

4. For the location of these root servers, see "Testimony of Michael M. Roberts, President and CEO, ICANN before the Senate Committee on Commerce, Science, and Transportation, Subcommittee on Communications," February 14, 2001, www.icann.org/correspondence/roberts-testimony-14feb01.htm [accessed March 20, 2003]. In January 2003, Espanix and the Internet Software Consortium announced their plan to jointly develop, install, and set up a root server in Madrid, Spain. See "Internet Software Consortium and Espanix to Jointly Deploy a Root Name Server in Spain," *Business Wire*, January 7, 2003.

5. See "ICP-3: A Unique, Authoritative Root for the DNS," July 9, 2001, www.icann.org/icp/icp-3.htm [accessed March 20, 2003] (noting that "from the inception of the DNS, its most fundamental design goal has been to provide the same answers to the same queries issued from any place on the Internet"). But see note 61 (discussing alternative root servers).

6. See Paul Mockapetris, "Domain Names—Concepts and Facilities" (Network Working Group, Request for Comments No. 882), November 1983, www.rfc-editor. org/rfc/rfc882.txt [accessed March 20, 2003].

7. See Jon Postel, "Assigned Numbers" (Network Working Group, Request for Comments No. 790), September 1981, www.rfc-editor.org/rfc/rfc790.txt [accessed March 20, 2003], and Vinton Cerf, "IAB Recommended Policy on Distributing Internet Identifier Assignment and IAB Recommended Policy Change to Internet 'Connected' Status" (Network Working Group, Request for Comments No. 1174), August 1990, www.rfc-editor.org/rfc/rfc1174.txt [accessed March 20, 2003]. IANA was first mentioned in RFC 1083 in 1988; see Internet Activities Board, "IAB Official Protocol Standards" (Network Working Group, Request for Comments No. 1083), December 1988, 9, www.rfc-editor.org/rfc/rfc1083.txt [accessed March 20, 2003].

8. For the dates of ccTLD delegations, see DNSO, ICANN, "History of the Internet: ccTLDs in Chronological Order of Top Level Domain Creation at the InterNIC," November 7, 2002, www.cctld.dnso.icann.org/ccwhois/cctld/ccTLDs-by-date.html [accessed March 20, 2003].

9. See Mueller, *Ruling the Root*, 88.

10. See Mueller, *Ruling the Root*, 88–89 (quoting Postel).

11. The list of ISO 3166-1 country codes is available at www.iso.ch/iso/en/prods-services/iso3166ma/02iso-3166-code-lists/list-en1.html [accessed March 20, 2003].

12. See John C. Klensin, "Reflections on the DNS, RFC 1591, and Categories of Domains" (Network Working Group, Request for Comments No. 3071), February 2001, 6 (hereinafter RFC 3071), www.rfc-editor.org/rfc/rfc3071.txt [accessed March 20, 2003] (stating that the .uk ccTLD predates the adoption of the ISO 3166-1 codes).

13. Examples of these ccTLDs include .ac (for Ascension Island), .gg (for Guernsey), .im (for the Isle of Man), and .je (for Jersey). See Kim G. von Arx and Gregory R. Hagen, "Sovereign Domains: A Declaration of Independence of ccTLDs from Foreign Control," *Richmond Journal of Law & Technology* 9, no. 1 (Fall 2002), www.law.richmond.edu/jolt/v9i1/article4.html, ¶ 40 n. 86 [accessed March 20, 2003]; see also RFC 3071, 6 (recognizing that these exceptions "are arguably, at least in retrospect, just mistakes").

14. Mueller, *Ruling the Root*, 89.

15. IANA, "ccTLD News Memo #1," October 23, 1997, www.iana.org/cctld/cctld-news1.htm [accessed March 20, 2003].

16. Mueller, *Ruling the Root*, 127.

17. Jon Postel, "Domain Name System Structure and Delegation" (Network Working Group, Request for Comments No. 1591), March 1994 (hereinafter RFC 1591), www.rfc-editor.org/rfc/rfc1591.txt [accessed March 20, 2003]; RFC stands for "Request for Comments." Although RFCs were sometimes published in final form, they generally "were intended to be an informal fast distribution way to share ideas with other network researchers"; see Leiner et al., "A Brief History of the Internet." As Don Mitchell described, the RFC process was a "sometimes brutal process of someone advancing an idea and everyone beating on it until the group consensus was that it would work"; see Mueller, *Ruling the Root*, 94 (quoting interview with Don Mitchell). Once consensus was achieved, the RFC would become an Internet standard until it was replaced by another RFC. For a detailed discussion of RFCs and Internet standard making, see generally A. Michael Froomkin, "Habermas@Discourse.Net: Toward a Critical Theory of Cyberspace," *Harvard Law Review* 116, no. 3 (January 2003): 749–873. As RFC 1718 stated, "There are . . . two special sub-series within the RFCs: FYIs and STDs. The For Your Information RFC sub-series was created to document overviews and topics which are introductory. . . . The STD RFC sub-series was created to identify those RFCs which do in fact specify Internet standards"; see IETF Secretariat et al., "The Tao of IETF: A Guide for New Attendees of the Internet Engineering Task Force" (Network Working Group, Request for Comments No. 1718), November 1994, 15, www.rfc-editor.org/rfc/rfc1718.txt [accessed March 20, 2003]. Thus, not all RFCs are Internet standards, although all Internet standards are RFCs.

18. All the ccTLD News Memos are available at www.iana.org/cctld/cctld-news. htm [accessed March 20, 2003]. The first memo appeared in October 1997. Four others were published in the next two years. The sixth memo came in October 2001, after a three-year hiatus. Released in the wake of the 2001 ICANN meeting in Los Angeles, this memo invited ccTLD managers to "initiate a bottom-up effort to assess and improve ccTLD registry security practices." Disappointedly, though, the Los Angeles conference focused primarily on online security issues as a result of the September 11, 2001, terrorist attacks and sidestepped important accountability and ccTLD matters; see Verne Kopytoff, "ICANN Forum Warns of Web Vulnerability," *San Francisco Chronicle*, November 17, 2001, B1. In February 2003, in the wake of its contract renewal with the DoC, IANA published its seventh memo, discussing internationalized, or multilingual, domain names and its ccTLD database.

19. IANA, "ccTLD News Memo #1."

20. Mueller, *Ruling the Root*, 127, 283 n. 31.

21. Kenneth Neil Cukier, "Eminent Domain: Initial Policy Perspectives on Nationalizing: Country-Code Internet Addresses," June 2002, 4, http://inet2002.org/CD-ROM/lu65rw2n/papers/g03-b.pdf [accessed March 20, 2003].

22. John S. Quarterman, "Haiti and Internet Governance," *Matrix News* 7, no. 5 (May 1997), www.mids.org/mn/705/ht.html [accessed March 20, 2003].

23. See "IANA Report on Request for Delegation of the .ps Top-Level Domain," IANA, March 22, 2000, www.icann.org/general/ps-report-22mar00.htm [accessed March 20, 2003].

24. See Arx and Hagen, "Sovereign Domains," ¶ 41, and Sergey Kuznetsov, "Russia May Say 'See Ya' to Dot-Su," *Wired News*, October 19, 2002, www.wired.com/news/print/0,1294,55687,00.html [accessed March 20, 2003].

25. The European Commission believed that the creation of the .eu domain was justified by "a decision by the ISO 3166 Maintenance Agency to extend the reservation of the existing EU code for the purposes of the Internet"; see European Commission, *The Creation of the .eu Internet Top Level Domain*, February 2, 2000, 5, http://europa.eu.int/comm/information_society/policy/internet/pdf/doteu_en.pdf [accessed March 20, 2003].

26. See Arx and Hagen, "Sovereign Domains," ¶ 42; see also ICANN, "Preliminary Report, Special Meeting of the Board," September 25, 2000, www.icann.org/minutes/prelim-report-25sep00.htm [accessed March 20, 2003].

27. For a discussion of the creation of the .eu ccTLD, see generally Arx and Hagen, "Sovereign Domains," ¶¶ 42–44.

28. For an excellent history of the U.S. government's efforts to privatize the DNS and early development of ICANN, see A. Michael Froomkin, "Wrong Turn in Cyberspace: Using ICANN to Route around the APA and the Constitution," *Duke Law Journal* 50, no. 1 (October 2000): 17–186. See also Jay P. Kesan and Rajiv C. Shah, "Fool Us Once Shame on You—Fool Us Twice Shame on Us: What We Can Learn from the Privatizations of the Internet Backbone Network and the Domain Name System," *Washington University Law Quarterly* 79, no. 1 (2001): 89–220.

29. "Improvement of Technical Management of Internet Names and Addresses," *Federal Register* 63 (February 20, 1998): 8826–33. The Green Paper is available at www.ntia.doc.gov/ntiahome/domainname/022098fedreg.htm [accessed March 20, 2003].

30. "Management of Internet Names and Addresses," *Federal Register* 63 (June 5, 1998): 31, 741–51. The White Paper is available at www.ntia.doc.gov/ntiahome/domainname/6_5_98dns.htm [accessed March 20, 2003].

31. WIPO, "The Management of Internet Names and Addresses: Intellectual Property Issues: Final Report of the WIPO Internet Domain Name Process" (Geneva: WIPO, 1999), 4. The final report of the First WIPO Internet Domain Name Process is available at wipo2.wipo.int/process1/report/index.html [accessed March 20, 2003].

32. Unfortunately, Postel died in October 1998 as a result of complications from open-heart surgery. As Professor Milton Mueller noted, "His death robbed the organization of its moral center, a good part of its institutional memory, and most of what remained of its legitimacy"; see Mueller, *Ruling the Root*, 181. For discussions and criticisms of ICANN, see generally James Boyle, "A Nondelegation Doctrine for the Digital Age," *Duke Law Journal* 50, no. 1 (October 2000): 5–16; Tamar Frankel, "The Managing Lawmaker in Cyberspace: A Power Model, *Brooklyn Journal of International Law* 27, no. 3 (2002): 859–902; Froomkin, "Habermas@Discourse," 838–55; Froomkin, "Wrong Turn in Cyberspace"; Joseph P. Liu, "Legitimacy and Authority in Internet Coordination: A Domain Name Case Study," *Indiana Law Journal* 74, no. 2 (Spring 1999): 587–626; Weinberg, "ICANN and the Problem of Legitimacy"; and Jonathan Zittrain, "ICANN: Between the Public and the Private—Comments before Congress," *Berkeley Technology Law Journal* 14, no. 3 (Fall 1999): 1071–93.

33. "Memorandum of Understanding between the U.S. Department of Commerce and Internet Corporation for Assigned Names and Numbers," November 25, 1998, www.ntia.doc.gov/ntiahome/domainname/icann-memorandum.htm [accessed March 20, 2003]. This agreement has since been amended a number of times. The amendments are available at www.ntia.doc.gov/ntiahome/domainname/icann.htm [accessed March 20, 2003].

34. "Contract between ICANN and the United States Government for Performance of the IANA Function," February 9, 2000, www.icann.org/general/iana-contract-09feb00.htm [accessed March 20, 2003].

35. Letter from J. Beckwith Burr, acting associate administrator for international affairs, National Telecommunications and Information Administration, U.S. Department of Commerce, to David Graves, director of business affairs, Network Solutions, Inc., February 26, 1999, www.ntia.doc.gov/ntiahome/domainname/icannnewco.htm [accessed March 20, 2003].

36. Froomkin, "Wrong Turn in Cyberspace," 70.

37. Some ICANN critics have pointed out that this formal structure existed merely on paper. It, however, did not exist in reality. In December 2002, ICANN reformed its organizational structure. Under the new structure, ICANN will have a

volunteer board of directors that includes fifteen voting and six nonvoting members, all of which will be selected by the three supporting organizations and ICANN's Nominating Committee. The Nominating Committee is composed of members selected by the supporting organizations, the advisory committees, and the board of directors. The three supporting organizations include the Generic Domain Name Supporting Organization (GNSO), the Address Supporting Organization (ASO), and the Country-Code Name Supporting Organization (ccNSO). In addition, ICANN is supported by the Governmental Advisory Committee, the At-Large Advisory Committee, the DNS Root Server System Advisory Committee, the Security and Stability Advisory Committee, and the Technical Liaison Group; see ICANN, "ICANN and the Global Internet," February 25, 2003, www.itu.int/itudoc/itu-t/workshop/cctld/024r1.html [accessed March 20, 2003]; see also ICANN, "ICANN and Reform," February 25, 2003, www.itu.int/itudoc/itu-t/workshop/cctld/025r1.html [accessed March 20, 2003].

38. ICANN, "ICANN and the Global Internet," 4.

39. IANA, "ICP-1: Internet Domain Name System Structure and Delegation" (ccTLD Administration and Delegation), May 1999, www.icann.org/icp/icp-1.htm [accessed March 20, 2003]. Although some commentators refer to ICP-1 as the "Internet Coordination Policy," the document stands for "ICANN Corporate Policy"; see ICANN, "Proposal to the U.S. Government to Perform the IANA Function," February 2, 2000, www.icann.org/general/iana-proposal-02feb00.htm [accessed March 20, 2003].

40. GAC, ICANN, "Principles for Delegation and Administration of ccTLDs Presented by Governmental Advisory Committee," February 23, 2000 (hereinafter GAC Principles), www.icann.org/committees/gac/gac-cctldprinciples-23feb00.htm [accessed March 20, 2003].

41. Mueller, *Ruling the Root*, 206. As the GAC Principles noted, "The relevant government or public authority ultimately represents the interests of the people of the country or territory for which the ccTLD has been delegated. Accordingly, the role of the relevant government or public authority is to ensure that the ccTLD is being administered in the public interest, whilst taking into consideration issues of public policy and relevant law and regulation" (GAC Principles § 5.1).

42. In 1997, Zaire changed its name to the Democratic Republic of the Congo. It has since occupied the .cd name space. See IANA, "Report on Deletion of the .zr Top-Level Domain," June 20, 2001, www.iana.org/reports/zr-report-20jun01.htm [accessed March 20, 2003].

43. Documents concerning the redelegation of these ccTLDs are available at www.iana.org/reports [accessed March 20, 2003].

44. Notably, ICANN did not enter into an agreement with NeuStar, the .us ccTLD manager. See Arx and Hagen, "Sovereign Domains," ¶ 37.

45. ICANN, "ccTLD Resource Materials," last updated January 13, 2003, www.icann.org/cctlds [accessed March 20, 2003].

46. See "Model ccTLD Sponsorship Agreement—Triangular Situation (Initial Version)," September 2, 2001, www.icann.org/cctlds/model-tscsa-02sep01.htm [ac-

cessed March 20, 2003]; see also Arx and Hagen, "Sovereign Domains," ¶¶ 32–34 (discussing ICANN's contractual powers).

47. Stuart Lynn, "ICANN, President's Report: ICANN—The Case for Reform," February 24, 2002, www.icann.org/general/lynn-reform-proposal-24feb02.htm [accessed March 20, 2003].

48. See ICANN, "ICANN and the Global Internet"; ICANN, "ICANN and Reform."

49. Cukier, "Eminent Domain," 2.

50. See Michael A. Geist, "ccTLD Governance Project," December 10, 2002, www.itu.int/itudoc/itu-t/workshop/cctld/cctld006.html [accessed March 20, 2003].

51. Arx and Hagen, "Sovereign Domains," ¶ 21.

52. Cukier, "Eminent Domain," 1. As Milton Mueller explained, "Just as the physical world was divided up into mutually exclusive territories controlled by sovereign governments, so could the name space be. Country codes were the most direct and obvious point of entry for this kind of thinking. If national governments could gain control over the assignment of their own country code, they could translate their geographic jurisdictions into cyberspace and gain a significant role for themselves in Internet governance" (Mueller, *Ruling the Root*, 205).

53. Cukier, "Eminent Domain," 1.

54. Kate Mackenzie, "Tuvalu's .tv Yields $88m," *The Australian*, January 29, 2002, 27.

55. See, for example, Akash Kapur, "United Nations vs. ICANN: One ccTLD at a Time," *CircleID*, January 29, 2003, www.circleid.com/articles/2564.asp [accessed March 20, 2003].

56. In March 2002, the government of South Africa introduced the Electronic Communications and Transactions Bill, which proposed to set up a new domain name authority within South Africa with board members chosen by the minister of communications. See Arx and Hagen, "Sovereign Domains," ¶ 23, and Geist, "ccTLD Governance Project."

57. Letter from Richard Alston, senator and minister for communications, information technology and the arts, Australia, to M. Stuart Lynn, president and chief executive officer, ICANN, July 4, 2001, www.iana.org/cctld/au/alston-to-lynn-04jul01.htm [accessed March 20, 2003].

58. Cukier, "Eminent Domain," 6 (see also 7–9, outlining a plan to nationalize ccTLDs).

59. See generally Roger A. Cunningham, William B. Stoebuck, and Dale A. Whitman, *The Law of Real Property*, 2d ed. (St. Paul, Minn.: West, 1993), 505–12, and *Nichols on Eminent Domain* (New York: Matthew Bender, 2003).

60. Cukier, "Eminent Domain," 6.

61. See Arx and Hagen, "Sovereign Domains," ¶ 83 (advocating the acknowledgment by national governments that each nation is authoritative for its respective ccTLD and the introduction of a peer-to-peer protocol into the DNS). Theoretically, any computers can resolve domain names by querying different name servers that point to different root servers. Alternative top-level domains and alternative root servers indeed exist. Nonetheless, very few computers look up domain names using

alternative root servers, and the vast majority rely on the set of thirteen "legacy" root servers to resolve domain names; see Mueller, *Ruling the Root*, 53–55, and Weinberg, "ICANN and the Problem of Legitimacy," 197–98.

62. The "WIPO ccTLD Best Practices for the Prevention and Resolution of Property Disputes" is available at http://ecommerce.wipo.int/domains/cctlds/bestpractices/index.html [accessed March 20, 2003]. The document is available in Arabic, Chinese, English, French, Spanish, and Russian.

63. The "Uniform Domain Name Dispute Resolution Policy" is available at www.icann.org/dndr/udrp/policy.htm [accessed March 20, 2003].

64. Under the UDRP, each registrant agrees to participate in a mandatory administrative proceeding when a third party complains to a dispute resolution service provider. The person bringing the case must then prove not only that the registrant's domain name is identical—or confusingly similar—to a trademark or service mark in which the complainant has rights but also that the person who registered the domain has no rights or legitimate interests to the domain name and that the domain name has been registered and is being used in bad faith.

65. Among the criticisms are the selection and composition of the dispute resolution panel, the failure to provide adequate time for a domain name registrant to reply to a complaint, the failure to ensure that the registrant has received actual notice of the complaint, and the registrant's limited access to courts for review when the dispute resolution panel decides against a party. For criticisms of the UDRP, see generally Michael Geist, "Fair.Com?: An Examination of the Allegations of Systemic Unfairness in the ICANN UDRP," *Brooklyn Journal of International Law* 27, no. 3 (2002): 903–37, and A. Michael Froomkin, "ICANN's 'Uniform Dispute Resolution Policy'—Causes and (Partial) Cures," *Brooklyn Law Review* 67, no. 3 (Spring 2002): 605–718. See also Laurence R. Helfer and Graeme B. Dinwoodie, "Designing Non-National Systems: The Case of the Uniform Domain Name Dispute Resolution Policy," *William and Mary Law Review* 43, no. 1 (October 2001): 141–274; Froomkin, "Wrong Turn in Cyberspace"; and Milton Mueller, "Rough Justice: An Analysis of ICANN's Uniform Dispute Resolution Policy," www.acm.org/usacm/IG/roughjustice.pdf [accessed March 20, 2003].

66. CENTR is an international association of ccTLD registries. CENTR provides a forum to discuss policy matters concerning ccTLD registries, acts as a channel of communication to Internet governing bodies and related organizations, and promotes the interests of not-for-profit ccTLDs by lobbying on their behalf. Although CENTR has a European focus, full membership is open to all ccTLD registries. Non-European members include CIRA (for Canada), IPM (for Iran), ISOC-IL (for Israel), and the Palestinian Registry. The website of CENTR is at www.centr.org.

67. Examples of these powerful ccTLD managers include Nominet UK (.uk) and DENIC (.de), each of which have millions of registrations. See Michael Geist, "Governments Hold Reins in Those National Domains," *Toronto Star*, March 10, 2003, D3.

∼

CHAPTER TWO

East Timor's .TP: From a Virtual Initiative to a Political Reality

Martin Maguire

When country code top-level domains (ccTLDs) were first delegated, few knew how they would evolve. While many ccTLDs were delegated in the mid-1980s and early 1990s, others sat dormant. It was not until May 1997 that East Timor's .tp was delegated to an Irish Internet Service Provider that sought to use the code to help bring freedom to the people of East Timor.

It was Martin Maguire who conceived of .tp as a virtual homeland and a tool for activism for the annexed East Timorese. Tracing the history of East Timor's ccTLD, he discusses activism, politics, and the inherent problems with the ccTLD naming system.

Like all Internet Service Providers (ISPs), my company, Connect-Ireland, is in the business of registering and setting up domain names and their associated services for clients. In a normal day, we register domains under .com, .net, and .org, as well as the Irish country code top-level domain (ccTLD), .ie, for people who wish to announce their Irish presence. Through this work, we learned about how domain registries are organized and the roles various organizations play in the politics and governance of the codes.

In 1997, we had a visit from Clement Dzidonu, a friend who had worked in the Department of Statistics at Dublin's Trinity College and was working at a college in Zimbabwe. Curious about domain names, Clement asked me to explain domain name registration and registries. The conversation highlighted aspects of the process that were not yet clear to me. He was curious why so many African country code domain name registries were, at that time, managed from various U.S. locations; I did not know the answer but agreed to find out.[1]

As part of our research, a member of our technical team, Declan Kelly (known as Dec), created various lists of domain names, including one listing of domains that had not yet been delegated. Though we were not quite sure how, we thought that there may be some value in the unused domains.

Dec pointed out that .tp, the code for East Timor (Timor-Portuguese), was one of the domain names that had yet to be delegated. It made me wonder, and I asked him to copy the list to me. The list sat on my desk for about three weeks. I realized that .tp would probably not be marketed as a "must have" domain name ending, like Tuvalu's .tv, which was marketed to television companies, but I thought that it might serve another purpose. The recent history of East Timor suggested to me that any action relating to .tp would have to have political connotations. I believed that the domain ending could assist the people of East Timor in their struggle against what was an internationally recognized but often publicly forgotten twenty-five-year struggle for independence.

East Timor forms part of a roughly crocodile-shaped island that lies approximately 500 kilometers (311 miles) north of Darwin, Australia.[2] This area first came to the attention of the West around 1515 during the age of exploration, when it became the object of dispute between the Dutch and the Portuguese.[3] The island was divided; the Portuguese inhabited East Timor, and the Dutch inhabited West Timor.

At the end of World War II, the Dutch and other colonial powers attempted to reclaim the Southeast Asian territories they once ruled. Indonesia, however, had declared independence. Under the leadership of Sukarno and Mohammad Hatta, the Indonesian people had a brutal war with the Dutch that lasted four years. When the United Nations intervened, the Dutch eventually agreed to withdraw from the area. This led to the formation of the Republic of Indonesia in November 1949. The newly formed republic inherited what had been known as the Dutch East Indies, including West Timor.

The Indonesians were able to win their independence from the Dutch, but East Timor was unable to win its independence from the Portuguese. As a result, in 1951, East Timor officially became an overseas province of Portugal; it was at this time that the .tp code qualified for the ISO 3166-1 directory. Being added to the list, which was first drafted in 1974, is significant because only the codes on the list are designated Internet ccTLDs.[4]

During the 1970s, Portugal was under the rule of the dictator Antonio de Oliveira Salazar.[5] On April 25, 1974, under the leadership of General Antonio de Spinola, the Portuguese military took control of Portugal. Soon after, Spinola declared that democratic rights would be accorded to the inhabitants of the Portuguese colonies in Africa and Asia, including East Timor.[6]

The liberalization caused instability in East Timor; there was a short civil war, but before a government could be established, with the tacit consent of the United States, Indonesia invaded in December 1975.[7]

During the next twenty-five years, it is estimated that more than 250,000 East Timorese citizens died at the hands of Indonesian military authorities.[8] As a proportion of the population, the death rate equals that of the Nazi Holocaust. East Timorese Bishop Carlos Belo wrote, "The Indonesian soldiery, which has robbed us of our freedom and destroyed our culture, treats us as scabby dogs. Justice is alien to them. The Indonesians keep us like slaves."[9]

When I saw that the ccTLD for East Timor had not yet been delegated, I believed that I could use the code to help liberate the people of East Timor. Recognizing that the first step was to obtain authority for the domain, I researched the rules relating to the delegation of ccTLDs. I contacted Tom Hyland of the East Timor–Ireland Solidarity Campaign (ETISC), for whom I had previously provided e-mail services and technical support.[10] Tom is a former Dublin bus driver; having seen a documentary on the atrocities in East Timor on local television, he gave up his job and set up the Irish campaign for East Timor. He was exceptional at gaining media coverage for East Timor, both in Ireland and abroad, and had become well known to the East Timorese leadership.

I determined that the Indonesian authorities had limited their use of .tp because they claimed that, as an entity, East Timor was merely another island of Indonesia. Tom shared our discussions with various members of the East Timorese leadership in exile, including the international independence campaign supporters, and Jose Ramos Horta, who, along with Bishop Belo, was a joint 1996 Nobel Peace Prize winner.

As I saw it, the domain registry had one potentially major value: to enable a political campaign. While .tp would require development, it could be useful in helping express both the historical injustices suffered by the East Timorese and their current struggles.

The Internet offered advantages for advocacy. The dispersed elements of the campaign for freedom could be gathered together, allowing for the creation and launch of the world's first "virtual" country. We decided that if it truly was, at that time, impossible to liberate East Timor, then the least we could do was to give the Internet community an opportunity to positively support the movement.

We first had to obtain the delegation of .tp. While the form was straightforward, there were several concerns to address. The primary document governing the establishment of ccTLDs, RFC 1591, required that domain name services be provided for the benefit of the local population; it also inferred duties on the registry to meet the needs of the wider Internet population[11] and required a local name, address, and contact details to be supplied.

We would have no problem meeting the first two requirements, but there were potential problems if we supplied the name and contact details of a contact person. Many thousands of East Timorese citizens had "disappeared" during the occupation by Indonesian forces; we were worried that by supplying personal details we would jeopardize the lives of the contact person, his or her family, or any residents at the stated address.[12]

I decided to provide the contact details of Xanana (pronounced "Sha-nana") Gusmão. Xanana was the East Timorese resistance leader who was incarcerated by the Indonesian authorities in Cipinang Prison in Jakarta, the Indonesian capital.[13] Xanana had already come to the attention of many of the world's leaders; South African President Nelson Mandela had arranged to visit him in Jakarta. We decided to list Xanana because his notoriety would provide him with a level of protection not available for the average citizen of East Timor.

I knew the name we would use but not the address, which was required to come from an individual or organization based within the country of application. The problem was how to do this quickly and easily. Tom told me that when Indonesian forces captured Xanana, he was taken to and held in the military commander's residence in Dili, East Timor's capital. I obtained the military commander's address in Dili and set out to establish, for my own piece of mind, that Indonesians did not and would not acknowledge the existence of East Timor.

I tried placing a call to the military commander's residence in East Timor. The call was routed to the Australian operator, but no matter how he expressed the destination, "Dili in East Timor," the Indonesian operators would not link the call because he used the term "East Timor." It confirmed to me that "East Timor" had been deemed a nonexisting entity and was expunged from the language by the Indonesian authorities.

Over several weeks, while discussing the project with Tom, I discovered that news of our potential activity was being discussed on several Internet e-mail lists that were run for the benefit of the East Timor international campaigns. Fearing that Indonesian authorities would apply for the delegation of .tp and prevent us from doing so, I immediately applied for the domain, using Xanana's name and the address in Dili where he had been under house arrest. Dec processed the application with the Internet Assigned Numbers Authority (IANA) and received an e-mail confirmation from Dr. Jon Postel.

We had the domain; now our task was to position it on the Internet and gain the support of the international East Timorese leadership and support groups. Our first act was the creation of a website using the domain name freedom.tp.[14] The design and layout of the site was intended to reflect the conditions in East Timor. It contained a number of potential actions, including national contact information, the creation of a virtual quilt, two downloadable screen savers, and an online petition.

In 1998, we set up the framework for the site and circulated the information via e-mail to most, if not all, of the international East Timor support organizations. Though the Internet was becoming more popular, it was still new to many people, including the social and political activists we contacted.

In response to my e-mail, I received many comments. Some were general questions, such as "Who are you?" and "Why are you involved?" Others questioned our decisions. "Why did you choose .tp?" one person asked. "This reflects the previous colonial power." While some questions were easy to answer, the question "Why .tp?" was extremely difficult to explain, particularly to people who had no idea of the design and evolution of the Internet.

The primary reason for using .tp was simply that we had no ability to choose; the ccTLDs were taken directly from the preestablished list known as the ISO 3166-1. The question "Why the ISO 3166-1 list?" is more complex; in fact, a close examination of the IANA ccTLD list shows several problems with using the ISO table for this purpose.

As discussed in RFC 1591, the ISO 3166-1 was chosen because it was a preexisting list of codes established according to a known procedure. Postel did not want IANA to be in the business of deciding what was and what was not a country.[15]

The ISO 3166-1 was not designed for use as ccTLDs; its purpose was to standardize country names into two-letter codes. In the beginning, the use of the list made sense—it was efficient. As the ccTLDs have become more valuable and more visible, however, the flaws of using the list as the model for ccTLDs have become more apparent.

For example, under the current system, several countries have more than one ccTLD under their control.[16] While in the early years this may not have appeared to matter, as governments take an increasing interest in ccTLDs, the number under their control could allow them to wield an unequal amount of power in the politics of the Internet.

China, for example, has control of several ccTLDs—China's .cn, Hong Kong's .hk, and Macau's .mo.[17] This authority stems from changes in international agreements between China and the former colonial powers. I am not inferring that China has abused or will abuse this position, but there is a potential that at some point in the future those nations with multiple domains will yield a greater representation and voting influence.

Another difficulty with using the ISO 3166-1 list is that it is constantly changing; the ISO (International Organization for Standardization) uses historical codes to identify events that may have occurred before a name changed. The Domain Name System, however, does not incorporate these historical codes; as a result, when a nation changes its name or dissolves, the prior code is intended to be replaced by the new code.[18]

When there are political changes, there is necessarily a time period when IANA's list of ccTLDs does not mirror the ISO 3166-1. After the Soviet Union dissolved, for example, it was just a matter of time before its code, .su, would be removed from the ISO 3166-1 and that the individual nations that emerged would be added.[19] However, while the Russian Federation, for example, was delegated its code, .ru, in 1994, the .su ccTLD was still up and running.[20] In a period of limbo, Ros NIIROS, the .su registrar, changed its policy to accept only third-level domain name registrations and did so for more than eight years.[21]

More recently, the discussion has regarded .yu, the ccTLD for Yugoslavia. The name of the country was officially changed to Serbia and Montenegro on February 4, 2003. The ISO noted that the process of determining a suitable code would take several weeks and recommended that those using .yu continue to do so until the new code elements are announced.[22]

This demonstrates the problems with IANA's one-way dependence on ISO codes. The IANA and, therefore, domain name registrants and Internet users are beholden to the ISO for their code choices and timetable.[23] Should Montenegro pursue its political autonomy, this entire process will once again have to be revisited.

The IANA's dependency on the ISO 3166-1 is also faulty because at certain times, in the case of .eu, for example, the IANA's rules are extended to allow a domain from a source other than the ISO 3166-1, primarily the ISO "Reserved Code Elements." This list was designed "to avoid transitional application problems and to aid users who require specific additional code elements for the functioning of their coding systems."[24]

In September 2000, the IANA noted that it had received various applications for the establishment of ccTLDs involving two-letter codes not on the ISO 3166-1 list but rather on the "Reserved List." The IANA recognized that "the delegability of such codes has varied from time to time in the past."[25] To reconcile the issue, it concluded that "codes not on the ISO 3166-1 list are delegable as ccTLDs only in cases where the ISO 3166 Maintenance Agency, on its exceptional reservation list, has issued a reservation of the code that covers any application of ISO 3166-1 that needs a coded representation in the name of the country, territory, or area involved."[26] The only code that fulfilled these requirements was .eu.

Regardless of whether those seeking the establishment of ccTLDs petition the ISO or the IANA, the practical effect is the same. Both groups are in an extremely powerful position; while the early appeal of the IANA's using the ISO table was its preestablished policies, as the Domain Name System has evolved, the policies have proved subject to political interests.[27]

Once the process of ccTLD delegation becomes subject of the will of the powerful, it can be misused. The result will be that only those who curry the right amount of favor can work their way into the ISO system and, therefore, the domain name hierarchy. Now that we are beyond the first wave of the Internet, it is time to make the tough decisions with the necessary transparency while providing access to independent authorities for review.

Surely, the intricacies of ccTLD naming were more than the East Timorese support groups sought to know in our initial communication; it was enough that they knew that .tp was the only code we could use. We agreed to launch the site in Dublin on November 11, 1998, a date nearest to the anniversary of the Santa Cruz massacre, and to begin an international press campaign shortly thereafter.[28]

During a trip to Vienna in January 1999, I received a note at my hotel telling me to immediately phone the office. When I did, I was informed that our Internet services had been attacked. I knew I had to get back to Ireland, but there I was, standing in a hotel room in Austria, two plane journeys away from home, with existing commitments. My staff and I agreed to handle the event over the telephone.

They had identified a serious denial-of-services attack whereby an attacker flooded our web server with false requests for information, overwhelming and crashing the system. My staff monitored the attack, which was seen as a protest to the launch of freedom.tp, while simultaneously trying to trace its source.

The breach of our security had extremely serious consequences for us as an ISP; we were offline. I first dictated a press release to issue to the Irish media and then authorized the purchase of new equipment. Work in Dublin commenced; our staff remained in the building and slept under desks when taking breaks.

After one day, I returned to the office to find that everything possible was being done. Disappointed that not a single media outlet published any information based on my press release, I rewrote and reissued it. Still there was no reaction from the media. I called Tom to discuss what had happened; he agreed to also contact the media.

By the next day, most of our services were back online; I replaced our own web home page with a copy of the press release. The next day, things began to change; on the front page of one of Ireland's largest national daily newspapers, the *Irish Examiner*, was an article that focused on the impact of the attack on local users.[29] The local BBC office in Dublin soon called to film a short video to use on its news and radio programs.

Despite the media attention to the local issues, we felt that the international scope of the issue was not fully understood by the local media. The publicity we were receiving incorrectly alluded to a website being hacked and missed the main issue: that it was not our website but the .tp ccTLD that had been targeted. We were considering how best to manage this issue with the media when we got a phone call from an Internet enthusiast in the United States; the message was quite simple: "Hi guys, you've probably been too busy to realize this, but your attack is now the biggest item on the web. You guys are the first Internet war!"

The six weeks that followed were a complete blur. Hits to our website and others relating to the attack reached 32 million in about two weeks. We received more than 14,000 e-mails of support; we eventually replied to each of them. I gave more than ninety press interviews in the following month. East Timor's struggle for independence was being covered in all media—newspapers, television, the Internet, and technical reviews. Even *New Scientist* devoted an entire page to the issue.[30] Politicians, including the U.S. secretary of state at that time, Madeleine Albright, were being interviewed and asked about the potential of terrorism on the Internet.

With a strange twist of fate, this media coverage far eclipsed anything that we had hoped to initiate with the plan to announce the launch of freedom.tp. It enabled us to realize our initial intention of publicizing the plight of the local inhabitants of East Timor. The activity with one simple press release had surpassed the activities that we were shortly going to launch. We were unsure of how beneficial all this sudden influx of publicity would be and how it would manifest in specific positive outcomes.

I soon realized the full impact of the raised profile of East Timor when someone showed me a *New York Times* article titled "East Timor Seems Suddenly to Be on Verge of Independence."[31] The article quoted the new Indonesian president, B. J. Habibie, as saying, "If someone asks me about East Timor, my suggestion is, give them freedom. It is just and fair."

The article said that Habibie's government was concerned about both the focus on Indonesia by human rights groups and the Asian economic crisis that caused Indonesia to need the financial support of the international community. The Indonesian government suddenly wanted to be rid of East Timor because freeing East Timor would relax the international scrutiny that was focused on Indonesia. "We don't want to be bothered by East Timor's problems anymore," Habibie added.

This statement was an indication of the extreme change in Indonesia's attitude; its former president, Suharto, who had resigned the previous May after more than three decades in power, insisted that East Timor would forever remain part of Indonesia.

Habibie ordered that Indonesia's foreign minister meet at the United Nations with his counterpart from Portugal, who was recognized by the United Nations as the territory's administrator, to discuss greater autonomy or independence for East Timor. The move worried many because of its intended speed, as East Timor might have found itself granted full independence before it was ready to govern itself and with the territory awash in guns.[32] Rights groups called on the Indonesian government to allow the United Nations to station monitors and possibly even peacekeeping troops in East Timor to observe a transition to independence and to prevent outbreaks of violence among East Timorese factions and the Indonesian military.

In an address, Albright said, "The stage has been set for a peaceful determination of East Timor's future. But the need now is for pragmatism and willingness to do hard work on transitional arrangements. For the goal must not be simply to slice East Timor apart or cast it adrift but rather to ensure its cohesion and viability—whether through autonomy or independence."[33]

Unfortunately, the expressions of Albright were not fully acted on by the Indonesian government; East Timor descended into a process of destabilization. Pro-Jakarta militias, believed to have been armed by factions of the withdrawing Indonesian military, attempted to intimidate voters. Regardless of this intimidation, the East Timorese voters retained their courage and voted by a four-to-one ratio for independence. This led several infuriated militias that were supporting the retention of the link with Indonesia to burn and destroy much of what remained of the country's infrastructure.[34]

The results of the actions in East Timor created a new focus on the position of the East Timorese people. This led, in time, to direct UN intervention in the form of a supervised referendum, the placing of UN-authorized peacekeeping forces in East Timor, and the release of political prisoners, including Xanana Gusmão.

The United Nations initiated the process with Secretary-General Kofi Annan's television and radio broadcasts to the East Timorese that explained that the referendum approved independence, thereby shaking off a quarter century of Indonesian rule over the former Portuguese colony. Under President Habibie, Indonesia's Golkar Party agreed that the August referendum was the best way to end the East Timorese conflict; the Indonesian national parliament approved the results before they became final.

The speed of the developments also took us, the East Timorese support groups, by surprise. In discussions, the best outcome had always been seen as being four to six years in the future. Suddenly, the virtual country would have to adapt to providing real services for people who would have equal freedom to communicate.

Discussing the news with Tom Hyland, we realized the greatest need would be for money to rebuild East Timor. I told Tom that I would activate and develop the East Timorese domain name space as an income stream.

The first task was to create the necessary infrastructure to provide a mass of .tp domain registrations. We had previously developed rules as part of the .tp action and had awarded domains to a number of individuals who had been active in supporting our initiative. The idea now was to promote the selling of .tp domain registrations and to use the funds to support the redevelopment of East Timor.

We began selling domains on a commercial basis and agreed to provide free domains and support services to any support group or organization that was actively involved in supporting or in working within East Timor. There is currently no real demand for the domain services from the indigenous population. In addition, Tom brought a number of East Timorese people to Ireland to introduce them to the Internet.

Our intention was to identify some younger East Timorese, pique their interests in computing, and train them to manage the domain registrations. Some have returned to East Timor and are now employed, while others have gained positions with international agencies. This, sadly, reflects the low educational status of the local East Timorese and reflects the latent demand for any East Timorese with a reasonable level of education.

Today, the long-term reconstruction of East Timor continues.[35] A large portion of the money that has been received from the international community was used for peacekeeping activities.

The lingering question for me was, "Can a domain registry assist in this process?" At first sight, it would appear that its ability would be limited. The new local telecommunications company has opened its doors, and we recently provided registration and services for the first government department to go online.[36]

The .tp domain identity, Timor-Portuguese, has caused some consternation among the recently elected parliament, which believes that the code reflects a colonial past. An application was made to the ISO to change the code to .tl, for "Timor Leste," which means, ironically, "East Timor" in Portuguese.[37] However, there are other, similar concerns over this new nomenclature.

We propose working with the East Timorese authorities in keeping the .tp domain and selling domain registrations to support the needs of East Timor on an ongoing basis. We want to erase .tp's connotation of colonization and replace it with notions of growth and development; .tp would connote "Tele-Phone." We want to set up a facility to register domains for a donation of $1.00 or more should the recipient wish to positively support the work of reconstruction. The idea is to construct a global contact directory.

For example, my old mobile telephone number was +353-85-8225563. I would have registered and set up a simple .tp website from a template. That page would list my contact information. So if you knew my phone number and you wanted to see my website or fax or mail me a letter, you would simply type in your browser "http://www.353858225563.tp."[38] The page could also be used to provide additional services to the user, potentially becoming a personal communications portal, with a range of communications options to mail, fax, and send instant messages. If the idea were supported, it would be one way to encourage web users to positively support one of the world's newest countries while also gaining communication benefits.

The registration fees would be given directly to East Timorese government and development agencies. The domain purchasers would be able to find out what local projects their registration funds were supporting. In addition, because this plan uses only the numerical .tp name space, it leaves the "word space" open to use for local community websites to claim once the infrastructure is built.

In a short period of time, what was seen as a "virtual" country supporting the many years of activist work suddenly became all too real. Planning for the domain was curbed by real-life events; we hope that our work added to the many actions over several decades and the ongoing international pressure. Like all actions of this type, there is an element of serendipity. At the height of the .tp publicity, a Canadian journalist asked me, "Could it not be that you planned all this?" My reply was simply, "I would like to think that we were that clever; unfortunately, we are not."

Notes

1. To answer the question, many ccTLDs had been divided up among U.S. agencies to administer until there were requests from local sources.

2. See Central Intelligence Agency, "East Timor," *World Factbook*, December 2002, www.cia.gov/cia/publications/factbook/geos/tt.html [accessed March 5, 2003].

3. For East Timor's history, see, for example, "A Brief History of East Timor," *East Timor Human Development Report 2002*, www.undp.east-timor.org/links%20for%20nhdr/annex%20-%20brief%20history%20of%20east%20Timor.pdf [accessed March 14, 2003].

4. The ISO 3166 was first published in December 1974. It listed about 220 "names of countries, dependencies and other areas of particular geopolitical interest." Most of the names in ISO 3166:1974 came from a list provided by the Statistical Office of the

United Nations; see "ISO Past, Present and Future," ISO, www.iso.ch/iso/en/prods-services/iso3166ma/04background-on-iso-3166/iso3166-past-present-and-future.html [accessed March 5, 2003].

5. See, for example, "Timeline: Portugal," BBC News, March 7, 2003, http://news.bbc.co.uk/1/hi/world/europe/1101811.stm [accessed March 14, 2003].

6. See, for example, "East Timor: Return of the Last Paradise," *The Jakarta Post*, www.thejakartapost.com/special/os_3_history2.asp#1, and www.dfa-deplu.go.id/english2/history.htm [accessed March 14, 2003].

7. See Noam Chomsky, "A Curtain of Ignorance," *Southeast Asia Chronicle* 74 (August 1980); see also Christopher Hitchens, *The Trial of Henry Kissinger* (New York: Verso, 2001).

8. See "East Timor: Birth of a Nation," Australian Broadcasting Corporation, www.abc.net.au/etimor/epis2.htm [accessed March 14, 2003].

9. Bishop Carlos Filipe Ximenes Belo, "They Keep Us Like Slaves," *Der Spiegel*, October 14, 1996, 165, translation at http://w3.rz-berlin.mpg.de/~wm/TIM/SPIEGEL_interview-E.html [accessed March 14, 2003].

10. See ETISC home page, www.freedom.tp/ireland/etisc [accessed March 5, 2003].

11. Jon Postel, "Domain Name System Structure and Delegation" (Network Working Group, Request for Comments No. 1591), March 1994, www.rfc-editor.org/rfc/rfc1591.txt [accessed March 13, 2003].

12. See, for example, "Indonesia and East Timor: Arms and Security Transfers Undermine Human Rights," Amnesty International, March 6, 1997, www.web.amnesty.org/ai.nsf/index/ASA210391997 [accessed March 14, 2003], and "The Struggle for East Timor," MoJo Wire, www.motherjones.com/east_timor [accessed March 14, 2003].

13. For more biographical details, see "Biography Xanana Gusmão," www.freedom.tp/people/xanana.htm [accessed March 14, 2003], and "Profile: Xanana Gusmão," BBC News, May 20, 2002, http://news.bbc.co.uk/1/hi/world/asia-pacific/342145.stm [accessed March 14, 2003].

14. See www.freedom.tp. This site has been "frozen" in time for historical purposes. As a result, the site is outdated, and many links do not function properly.

15. See note 11.

16. See, for example, "Country Codes," www.sandcollection.de/country-code.htm [accessed March 14, 2003].

17. See CNNIC's .cn at www.cnnic.com.cn, MONIC's .mo at www.monic.net.mo, and HKIRC's .hk at www.hkirc.net.hk/hkdnr/index.jsp [each accessed March 14, 2003].

18. See, for example, Zaire's .zr. When Zaire became the Democratic Republic of the Congo, its code became .cd; see "The dot CD Registry," www.cd [accessed March 14, 2003]. .zr ceased to be listed on the ISO 3166-1 in 1997, but the ccTLD was not deleted until 2001.

19. Interestingly, only thirteen of the fifteen independent nations received new codes; for historical reasons, two nations, Belarus and Ukraine, were already listed on the ISO 3166-1. When the United Nations was founded in 1945, each member nation was allocated one voice and one vote in the General Assembly. When this

rule was applied to the huge Soviet Union, this was felt to be unfair and a potential cause for future political problems. To remedy this situation at least to some extent, Ukraine and (the then) Byelorussia were admitted as full voting members and, thereby, given their own ISO 3166-1 codes. See "ISO Bulletin," ISO, April 2000, 11, www.iso.ch/iso/en/commcentre/pdf/Codes0004.pdf [accessed March 14, 2003].

20. See Sergey Kuznetsov, "Russia May Say 'See Ya' to Dot-Su," *Wired News*, October 19, 2002, www.wired.com/news/technology/0,1282,55687,00.html [accessed March 14, 2003].

21. As of May 2002, there were more than 28,000 domain names registered; many called for the .su name space to live despite its earlier removal from the ISO 3166-1 list. See note 20.

22. "Information on Serbia and Montenegro," ISO, February 6, 2003, www.iso.org/iso/en/prods-services/iso3166ma/01whats-new/2003-02-06_statement_yu.html [accessed March 14, 2003].

23. See Ivana Pavlovic, "Yugoslavia Top Level Domain Name Quandary," europe-media.net, February 26, 2003, www.europemedia.net/shownews.asp?ArticleID=15127 [accessed March 19, 2003].

24. For the list of reserved codes, see "ISO 3166 Reserved Codes," www.crwflags.com/fotw/flags/iso3166r.html [accessed March 18, 2003]; for background on the reserved codes, see "Reserved Code Elements," ISO, www.iso.ch/iso/en/prods-services/iso3166ma/04background-on-iso-3166/reserved-and-user-assigned-codes.html#reserved [accessed March 18, 2003].

25. "Preliminary Report, Special Meeting of the Board," ICANN, September 25, 2000, www.icann.org/minutes/prelim-report-25sep00.htm. Often called "mistakes," the ccTLDs for Ascension Island (.ac), Guernsey (.gg), Isle of Man (.im), and Jersey (.je), for example, were delegated while the codes were on the "Reserved List"; see John C. Klensin, "RFC 3071: Reflections on the DNS, RFC 1591, and Categories of Domains" (Network Working Group, Request for Comments No. 3071), February 2001, www.rfc-editor.org/rfc/rfc3071.txt [accessed March 13, 2003].

26. See note 25.

27. Why, for example, does the European Union get a code but not Tibet or Scotland?

28. On November 12, 1991, Indonesian troops fired on what began as a peaceful memorial procession to a cemetery in Dili, East Timor, and had turned into a proindependence demonstration. More than 271 East Timorese died of their injuries; see, for example, East Timor Action Agency, "The Santa Cruz Massacre," www.etan.org/timor/SntaCRUZ.htm [accessed March 18, 2003].

29. Caroline O'Doherty, "Terroris[t] Attack by Hackers Hits Firms," *Irish Examiner*, January 23, 1999, http://archives.tcm.ie/irishexaminer/1999/01/23/ihead.htm [accessed March 18, 2003].

30. See, for example, "Virtual Warfare," *New Scientist*, February 27, 1999, 51; see also Bob Paquin, "Jakarta Blamed for Cyber Warfare Attack on Dili Site," *The Straits Times* (Singapore), February 12, 1999, 24; "Trouble in E-Timor," *Asiaweek*, February 5, 1999, 59; and "Indonesia, Ireland in Info War?" *Wired News*, January 27, 1999, www.wired.com/news/politics/0,1283,17562,00.html [accessed March 14, 2003].

31. See Philip Shenon, "East Timor Seems Suddenly to Be on Verge of Independence," *New York Times*, February 18, 1999, A4.

32. See Shenon, "East Timor Seems Suddenly to Be on Verge of Independence," noting, "In a statement in Congress, Stanley Roth, assistant secretary of state for East Asian and Pacific affairs said the State Department had received 'numerous reports that the Indonesian army has been arming' anti-independence militia groups in East Timor, adding that the United States welcomed a recent statement by the Indonesian government that it would support an effort to disarm the groups before a withdrawal of Indonesian troops."

33. See Secretary of State Madeleine K. Albright, "Indonesia, the United States and Democracy," March 5, 1999, http://secretary.state.gov/www/statements/1999/990305a.html [accessed March 14, 2003].

34. "Unfinished Business: Justice for East Timor," *Human Rights Watch*, August 2000, www.hrw.org/backgrounder/asia/timor/etimor-back0829.htm [accessed March 14, 2003].

35. For current news, see "East Timor: Emerging Nation," Radio Australia, www.abc.net.au/asiapacific/specials/etimor/default.htm [accessed March 14, 2003].

36. See Ministry of Foreign Affairs and Cooperation–East Timor home page, www.mfac.gov.tp [accessed March 19, 2003].

37. "Change of Names and Alphabetical Code Elements of East Timor," *ISO 3166-1 Newsletter* 5, no. 5 (May 20, 2002), www.iso.ch/iso/en/prods-services/iso3166ma/03updates-on-iso-3166/nlv5e-tl.html [accessed March 14, 2003].

38. Try this address; you will see a dummy page with my contact details.

~

CHAPTER THREE

Chile's .CL: A Virtual Home for Chileans Worldwide

Patricio Poblete

For almost twenty years, the nation of Chile was governed by military rule. While the dictatorship brutally silenced political opponents, it also instituted liberal economic policies. As a result, Chile was not closed off from the global technological advances occurring in the 1970s and 1980s.

In 1987, on behalf of the University of Chile, Patricio Poblete and his colleagues were delegated the authority to administer .cl, the country code top-level domain for Chile. Crediting the early start, responsive rule making, and a sense of national identity, Poblete has seen the .cl name space become the most popular domain name ending for the Chilean people.

Located at the southern end of South America, a long and narrow strip of land to the west of the Andes, Chile was an early adopter of the Internet. The effect of that early start on the use of domain names can now be seen everywhere in the country. Chilean billboards, newspaper ads, television shows, and delivery vans carry Internet addresses that end in .cl. The early use of Chile's country code top-level domain (ccTLD), .cl, solidified a national understanding and appreciation for Chile's own space on the Internet. The result is that, to this day, Chileans use .cl more than any other Internet address ending.

Most Chileans take for granted that their favorite stores, magazines, and television shows have a website address ending in .cl. The result is that Chile, with 15 million inhabitants, has more domain names registered under its ccTLD than many other, much larger nations. In mid-February 2002,

31

Chile had 83,329 registered domain names; Spain, with a population of 40 million, had 44,398 domains within the .es name space; and Mexico, with a population of 100 million, had 75,357.[1]

Although it is hard to find estimates of the number of .com registrations from Chile, the sites indexed by local search engine TodoCL give a good indication.[2] While TodoCL indexed a total of 20,457 sites located in Chile that have .cl addresses, it found only 635 sites with .com addresses that are based in Chile. This difference in numbers proves that those who publish websites in Chile choose to do so primarily in the .cl name space. In addition to the high number of locally hosted .cl addresses, the index also notes that there are 13,334 sites with .cl addresses that are located outside Chile.[3] The registrants for such foreign-based .cl sites are likely to be individuals and Chilean companies who are using web-hosting services in North America plus foreign companies that are looking to appeal to the Chilean audience.[4] A number of technological, political, and cultural factors have contributed to the high number of .cl registrations, and I explore many of these in this chapter.

In the mid-1980s, Chile was still known to the world primarily because of news updates that would remind people that General Augusto Pinochet, who had seized power in Chile in a bloody coup in 1973, was still in power and facing increasing opposition from the Chilean population. One of the institutions that had stubbornly refused to yield to the dictates of the military regime was the University of Chile, the oldest and largest university in the country and often a source of headaches for the government.

Despite the firing of many left-wing academics and the appointment of military rectors, many of the remaining academics were still very critical of the regime; so, too, were the students. By the early 1980s, when political repression softened a bit and worsening economic conditions prompted a large part of the population to protest openly, the university had become a focal point for the opposition. In spite of the political environment, the university remained a leading research institution, with many of its young researchers traveling to North America for their graduate studies. It became natural that the university should be where the first experiments with international computer networking were made.

While the Pinochet dictatorship used heavy-handed repression to silence and neutralize political opponents, it was very liberal in its handling of the economy, promoting exports and lowering tariffs for imports. This had a positive impact on the availability of up-to-date technology. After the deep economic crisis of the early 1980s, the economy started a steady recovery. By the time the dictatorship was replaced by a democratically elected government in 1989, the conditions were ripe for the country to join the group of nations already connected to the Internet. The change in government happened when Pinochet, who had already been in power for fifteen years, lost a crucial referendum that would have extended his term for another eight years. One year after his defeat, the opposition candidate, Patricio Aylwin, won an open election. Pinochet did not go away completely, though. Under the terms of his 1980 constitution, he remained head of the army for another eight years.

Chile's experience with international networking had started some years earlier. In 1984, a group of researchers in the University of Chile's Department of Computer Science had already begun exchanging e-mail with other local universities, using modems and dial-up connections with the UUCP (Unix to Unix Copy Program) network. By today's standards, this was a rudimentary and painfully slow method for transmitting files over telephone lines, but it was sufficient to carry e-mail and online bulletin boards called Usenet newsgroups among many computers. Building on the network, a couple of years later the first experiments with international e-mail exchange were conducted with the help of France's National Institute for Computer Science and Automation Research (INRIA). E-mail became a permanent service in 1987 with the help of UUNET, a company that had just been formed and that would later become one of the largest commercial Internet Services Providers (ISPs) in the world.

To make communication on the network less technically burdensome, domain names had recently been developed by the Internet engineers. When we attempted to register uchile.cl, the domain name for the University of Chile, we discovered that Chile's ccTLD, .cl, had not yet been assigned to anyone's authority. It had already been decided that each country was going to be assigned its own two-letter code, but at the time most of the codes did not have an appointed administrator. The positions were being filled as the need arose.

As a result, we, like computer scientists in many other countries, had to do it ourselves. In the beginning, the responsibility of managing a top-level domain often fell to the local Internet pioneers, be they university researchers, research foundations, or early Internet entrepreneurs. We therefore assumed the task of maintaining the list of domain names under .cl. At that time, none of us imagined the extent to which this list would grow over the years and that at the beginning of the twenty-first century we would be managing a critical component of the network infrastructure for the country.

For several years, network access from Chile consisted mainly of e-mail service plus some Usenet newsgroups. The University of Chile was also instrumental in the development in Chile of BITNET, one of the world's earliest computer networks, consisting mainly of IBM mainframes. The network connection was set up in 1988 by the University of Chile, with the help of the U.S. National Aeronautics and Space Administration (NASA). The network connected to many universities in the United States, Canada, and Europe and extended later to other countries in Latin America. With access to a dedicated link, BITNET carried most of the international traffic, but it was the other UUCP network that made domain-style addresses known and popular among students. It is these students who would be the moving force in the next wave of the networking revolution.

Because the BITNET link was provided as part of an academic project, there were restrictions on its use for commercial purposes. Our other network, UUCP, on the other hand, had no such constraints. As a result, besides the universities, several companies and individuals also started using this new communication medium and registering their domain names.

It was at that time that we made an important decision with regard to the structure of the .cl name space. We were aware that some ccTLD administrators subdivided their address spaces using the same type of scheme used for the generic top-level domains. For example, where .xy is a ccTLD, one would see companies using domains of the form "name.com.xy" or universities using "name.edu.xy." Other countries, however, were not subdividing the space, and everyone could register directly under the ccTLD; in these countries, addresses were shorter since they took the form "name.xy."

We decided to join this second camp. Although we recognized that a common space might cause more domain name conflicts, we also saw that the usual subdivision often generated a very skewed distribution. We found that, when subdivided, most names are registered under .com.[5] If there were very few names registered in other second-level domains, then there would be the same conflicts; in this case, they would be under .com.cl as opposed to just .cl. Using this rationale, we found that not much was lost by not subdividing, and we were swayed by the ease of the shorter addresses.

This may have played an important role in the widespread adoption of .cl that occurred years later. In the Chilean people's minds, just as foreign domain names usually ended in .com, Chilean ones were supposed to end in .cl. They already had all the universities as examples of that plus a few local companies that were beginning to test the waters of this new medium.

The prehistoric era of networking based on both UUCP and BITNET began to fade in early 1992, when Chile was linked to the global Internet through the high-speed National Science Foundation Network (NSFNET). It was the policy of NSFNET to allow only one Internet link per country; unfortunately, this edict was not enough to force all the Chilean universities to agree. Bowing to university politics, they split into two competing consortia.[6] REUNA (Red Universitaria Nacional) consisted of nineteen public and semiprivate universities that included the University of Chile and most other universities. Unired, which was later renamed Red de Computadores (RdC), or Computer Network, was formed by three other universities. After several months, NSFNET allowed each consortium to operate its own independent link to become an ISP. A frantic and, at times, bitter race started between them; it ended when both groups connected to the Internet within hours of each other in 1992.[7]

The fierce competition between the groups had the beneficial effect of publicizing the Internet in Chile. The media attention was welcome because each of the providers hoped that enlisting commercial customers would help finance their operations.[8] The fact that both providers adopted names in the .cl name space, in turn, helped this suffix become better known among possible customers.[9]

In the early days of REUNA and Unired/RdC, the administration of the domain name registry remained in the Department of Computer Science of the University of Chile. The registry, which was named "NIC Chile," was left in the university's control despite pressure by the university's administration that wished it to be handed over to REUNA. The administration wanted REUNA to become stronger. It thought that it could control REUNA and, through it, regain control over the many regional universities that in former years had been part of the University of Chile but were now independent entities. The regional universities were happy to let the University of Chile foot a large part of the bill for REUNA but insisted on "one university, one vote" at the time of making political decisions.

While the central administration wanted to make REUNA stronger in its fight against Unired/RdC, the managers of the NIC Chile registry wanted to ensure that it remained a neutral service—which was mandated by RFC 1591.[10] The University of Chile was (and continues to be) a large and diverse institution; because the registry was located in the influential Faculty of Engineering, it was somewhat insulated from the political decisions of the administration.[11] The result of this was that, during confrontational times between REUNA and Unired/RdC, the registry continued to provide service in a fair manner to all customers. Instead of involving itself with the political disputes of the day, the registry concentrated on guaranteeing the technical operation of the Domain Name System; as a result, it gained respect among the Chilean technical community that continues to this day.

In the mid-1990s, there was a quick growth in both the number of Internet users and the number of Internet hosts in Chile and around the world; the recently introduced World Wide Web fueled the expansion.[12] Students who developed many of the early websites also became the early adopters and the main evangelists for the new technology. While these students were familiar with the taxonomy of domain names in use around the world, when it came to websites with local content, they had matured using Internet addresses that ended in .cl. For them, it was natural that their new websites also had names ending with the same suffix.

NIC Chile operated without written rules. It followed domain name pioneer Jon Postel's basic rule—"Be fair"—and trusted that users would use the service in good faith.[13] However, by 1997 the number of registered domain names under .cl had climbed to about 1,000, and NIC Chile needed to develop automated registration interfaces to handle the increased number of registrations. An informal group of interested people, most of them attorneys, started meeting to discuss formal domain name registration rules and to develop policies to resolve the conflicts that inevitably would arise among people competing for the same domain name.

The attorneys soon drafted a set of rules. A person would apply for a domain name with NIC Chile. A list of pending domain names was published on NIC Chile's website. Those who believed that they had more rights to the name and wanted to oppose a domain name application had one month from the application date to submit a claim to the domain. If the month passed without objection, the registrant would pay the registration fee, and the process was complete. Conflicts that arose through this process would be solved by arbitration that would be provided by the Santiago Chamber of Commerce's Mediation and Arbitration Center.

The basic idea was that there should be a simple, inexpensive, and efficient way for disputes to be raised and settled. Because the court system in Chile is notoriously slow, arbitration was seen as a good alternative.

The rules were specifically framed to ensure that NIC Chile did not have the authority to ban names or to make a prior assessment of names being applied for; this strengthened NIC Chile's position as a neutral manager whose role was limited to providing a dispute resolution mechanism. The general philosophy would continue to be to allow domain names to be registered and to rely on the dispute resolution system to solve conflicts when they appeared.[14]

This attitude of minimizing a priori regulations and fixing problems if and when they happened is not very typical of Chile. We believed that it was the right thing to do and were able to use the general laissez-faire culture of the Internet as leverage to have people accept it. Many critics, particularly lawyers and politicians, called for much a stronger prior assessment before authorizing a domain name to be registered. This was the path that countries like Spain and France took; in each of these cases, the decision led to much less use of their respective ccTLDs.[15] We managed to get away with a system in which you could register anything, but the key to having it accepted was to have a reliable dispute resolution procedure so that conflicts would be solved and piracy attempts stopped.

By September 1997, this draft set of rules was well on its way to becoming the new policy for .cl when something unexpected happened. On a typical day, the domain name registration inbox received only a few applications, but on one particular day it was flooded with applications from only two customers. In a few days, several thousand domain names had been requested; even a cursory inspection of the list revealed that it contained mostly well-known names of businesses and trademarks in Chile.

The local press quickly reported the news. It was at this point that most of the Chilean people learned about both of the existence of the Internet and of a new phenomenon called cybersquatting. A person becomes a cybersquatter when he or she registers or uses a domain name with a bad-faith intent to profit from the goodwill of a trademark belonging to someone else.

NIC Chile's reaction was to quickly put in place the draft rules and begin charging for domain name registrations. The rules would apply not only to new applications but also to those already in the pipeline. Because the rules were implemented, the few thousand domain names requested would cost some money to register, and the companies known by those names would have a way to fight back for them.

In practice, this meant that most of the initial thousands of domain name applications were eventually invalidated because payment was never received. It also resulted in an increase in the number of registrations by companies that felt threatened by possible cybersquatters. While the number of possible lawsuits went up when many of the traditional law offices discovered the trademark implications of the Internet and domain names, it was significant that NIC Chile was still managed by Internet pioneers. We recognized that domain names could collide with trademarks but that they were really different. We understood that non–trademark holders could have a legitimate right to register a domain name and that there was no automatic right for trademark holders to have domain names assigned to them.

Shortly after the Chilean arbitration-based dispute resolution system was introduced in 1997, we received complaints about the excessive cost and lack of specialization of the Santiago Chamber of Commerce's arbitrators. Therefore, NIC Chile, working jointly with the Chilean Association for Industrial Property, appointed a group of arbitrators who were cheaper and had a demonstrated knowledge of the Internet and domain names. The new system worked very well; it has also been recently improved by holding public applications to join the group of arbitrators, with a selection committee composed of a wide range of members of the Internet and legal communities. The Chilean undersecretary of telecommunications, who represents

Chile in the Internet Corporation of Assigned Names and Numbers (ICANN) Governmental Advisory Committee (GAC), and the Chilean undersecretary of economy, who is charged with the development of the information economy, oversee the process. This kind of transparent, open process to appoint arbitrators has been important in strengthening the acceptance of the dispute resolution system in the local community.

The dispute resolution system has evolved to adapt to the requirements of the community. The original system allowed those who believed that they were more entitled to a domain to file a claim for the domain within one month of the registrant's filing of the application. This often solved the problem of cybersquatting because the cybersquatter—who had not yet paid for the domain—would abandon the registration process as soon as someone else entered a claim to the domain.

While maintaining the one-month time line, the current system is supplemented by a process like the Uniform Dispute Resolution Policy (UDRP) that allows domain names to be disputed beyond the initial month.[16] If a claim is brought in the first month, the domain is granted to the person with the most rights to the name; if a claim is brought after the first month, the person complaining has a greater burden of proof and must prove not only that he or she is more entitled to the name but also that the domain was registered in bad faith.

We decided to incorporate both processes into our system because the community values having a successful lightweight system that can be applied quickly when a cybersquatting attempt is discovered in progress, and latecomers value the fact that they can file a complaint under the UDRP-style system, even though, in that case, they bear a heavier burden of proof.

Although many of the arbitrators are lawyers who come from the intellectual property camp, their decisions do not show a strong bias toward awarding the domain names to the complainants, who are often trademark owners. A mid-2002 study of published decisions found that decisions favored the complainant in 51 percent of the cases and the original domain holder in 49 percent of them.[17]

Since 1997, there has been a steady increase in the number of registered domain names in the .cl name space. In early 2003, the number of .cl domain names had risen to more than 80,000.[18] While since the .com boom the number of new registrations has diminished, the number of registrations has remained higher than the number of domain names that are not renewed. This keeps the total number of registered domains from decreasing. From a funding point of view, this has been important for NIC Chile because it has allowed the price of domain name registration and renewal to be kept low compared to international standards.

A 2002 NIC Chile study, conducted with the help of Latin American ccTLD administrators, found that every Latin American country charges for domain names except for Argentina and El Salvador. Charging just under U.S.$28 for a two-year registration, Chile had, at the time, the lowest fees in Latin America.[19] This is less than half the price of a .com domain. While people found it natural to register under .cl, if the price had been much higher than .com (instead of the other way around, as it is), they certainly would have done more research and discovered that there was really no technical reason to prefer one domain over the other. With low prices, they had little reason to innovate. There is also the convenience of having a registration service that is located in the country because it does business in the local currency and in the local language, and people can phone or even go to the office in person if they have problems. Chilean customers, most of whom speak only Spanish and are wary of using credit cards to make telephone and online purchases, had none of the local conveniences if they registered under .com.

In 1999, ICANN met in Santiago; this marked another milestone for the recognition of the Internet and the Domain Name System in Chile. The meeting was attended by a small but active group of members of the Chilean Internet community and marked the beginning of the participation of several Chileans in the various councils and committees of ICANN. It was also the first time that representatives of the Chilean government attended the exclusive GAC meetings and became interested in matters of Internet governance. Chile has been one of the frequent participants in GAC meetings ever since.

Even though some government officials had become involved in ICANN, it was not until September 2000 that the Domain Name System became a hot topic for Chilean politicians. It was then that two members of parliament held a press conference and denounced what they understood as abuses committed by NIC Chile. In essence, they blamed NIC Chile for all instances of alleged or actual cybersquatting of Chilean trademarked names or names that were otherwise recognizably Chilean, both under .cl and under .com, for which NIC Chile had absolutely no authority at all.

Sadly, this display is typical of the way some Chilean politicians approach their tasks. Because some give such priority to the public relations value of their actions, people often distrust what politicians say. Despite the distrust, however, people also tend to believe that if something bad is being said about someone—like NIC Chile in this case—then there must also be some truth in the claim.

The ensuing public scandal filled many pages in the local press and caused an investigative committee to be appointed in the Chamber of Deputies. It was quickly understood that NIC Chile had nothing at all to do with cyber-squatting .com domains, but it took longer for it to be accepted that, even when a perceived abusive domain was registered under .cl, it was not the registry's responsibility to detect it and reassign the name. It was not easy for deputies and senators to understand that NIC Chile was not acting as an authority that received applications for domain names and decided which ones to accept and which ones to deny but that it was simply a registration service where anyone could register names as long as no one else complained.

Among all the cases that were mentioned by the critics, the one that probably had the biggest public impact was that of "chile.cl." This domain name had been registered by a nonprofit foundation with the written blessing of the Ministry of Economy in 1996, which was before the registration rules were formalized. It had been used as the name for a site for information about the regions of Chile until early 2000, when it was sold by the foundation to a private group that was also the holder of "chile.com." The members of parliament who held the press conference mentioned chile.cl as the prime example of NIC Chile misbehavior because in their view this name should have been assigned only to the government.[20]

NIC Chile's system required no prior assessment and favored the use of a dispute resolution procedure in case of complaints. To this date, many words have been devoted to this issue.[21] Yet, no complaint has been formally filed under the dispute resolution system, nor has any suit been brought under the Chilean courts, so the final outcome of such a case remains a matter of speculation.

Even though the Chilean domain name registration system is widely supported by the community, until a couple of years ago there was no formal mechanism for the community to participate in the creation of policies. As a first step to solving this problem, an advisory board was established. This board, which is composed of community groups, individuals, and government ministries involved with Internet policy, has reviewed all changes of policy that have occurred and has approved the mechanism for the appointment of new arbitrators. For NIC Chile, this was a very pragmatic thing to do: if customers believe that they have no way to influence the policies of NIC Chile, they might be inclined to call for someone else to take over this function, so participation is necessary if the system is to be stable. However, having participation by the individual users has so far remained hard, as the organizations that purport to represent them tend to be very small, and many people doubt their claims to represent the community as a whole. The concept of an advisory board will probably be strengthened by giving it the force of an official government decree. Under this proposed rule, NIC Chile would act as the secretariat for this new body, which would operate under the name National Council for Domain Names and Internet Addresses.

Both the cultural evolution and the technological infrastructure of Chile have provided for high use of the .cl name space. The early start, low-price, and low-hassle registration as well as the Chilean culture's sense of national identity have led to high participation in .cl. The result of this confluence is the evolution of .cl from an unmanaged, unregulated name space to a more orderly, participatory online home for the Chilean people.

Notes

1. For up-to-date Mexican registration statistics, see Nic-México at www.nic.mx/nic/plsql/nic.nic_IniEst?X=0&Y=0 [accessed March 13, 2003]; for Spain's registration statistics, see ES-NIC at www.nic.es/estadisticas/index.html [accessed March 13, 2003]; for Chile's registration statistics, see NIC Chile at www.nic.cl/stat.html [accessed March 13, 2003].

2. See TodoCL at www.todocl.cl [accessed March 13, 2003].

3. Ricardo Baeza-Yates, Barbara J. Poblete, and Felipe Saint-Jean, "Estudio de la Web Chilena 2001-2001," www.todocl.cl/stats/estudio2002.pdf [accessed March 18, 2003].

4. As an example of the latter, see Google Chile at www.google.cl [accessed March 13, 2003].

5. This is often true to this day. For example, Brazil has more than fifty second-level domains, including some like "tv.br" for television stations and "eng.br" for engineers. Statistics show that more than 91 percent of all Brazilian registrations fall under "com.br"; see Registro.br at http://registro.br/estatisticas.html [accessed March 13, 2003].

6. See, for example, Eric Roberts, "Pricing of the Internet: Chile," 1998, www-cse.stanford.edu/classes/cs201/projects-97-98/pricing-of-the-internet-1/chile.htm [accessed March 20, 2003].

7. Ricardo Baeza-Yates, José M. Piquer, and Patricio V. Poblete, "The Chilean Internet Connection or I Never Promised You a Rose Garden," Proceedings INET'93, www.nic.cl/inet93/paper.html [accessed March 13, 2003].

8. Florencio I. Utreras, "REUNA: How an Academic Network Can Be Self Funded," May 10, 1995, www.isoc.org/HMP/PAPER/121/html/paper.html [accessed March 13, 2003].

9. See REUNA at www.reuna.cl [accessed March 13, 2003]; see also RdC (which is now owned by AT&T Latin America) at www.rdc.cl [accessed March 13, 2003].

10. Jon Postel, "Domain Name System Structure and Delegation" (Network Working Group, Request for Comments No. 1591), March 1994, www.ietf.org/rfc/rfc1591.txt [accessed March 13, 2003].

11. The Faculty of Engineering was financially stronger than the rest of the university and had more clout in terms of research. This allowed it to say no to some of the wishes of the central administration.

12. See Tim Berners-Lee, *Weaving the Web: The Original Design and Ultimate Destiny of the World Wide Web* (New York: HarperCollins, 2000).

13. See, for example, "Interview with Jon Postel," *OnTheInternet*, September 1996, http://oceanpark.com/papers/postel.html [accessed March 13, 2003].

14. José M. Piquer and Patricio V. Poblete, "Domain Name Conflict Resolution under the .CL Top-Level Domain," Proceedings INET'99, www.nic.cl/Charlas/INET99 [accessed March 13, 2003].

15. According to AFNIC's "Nombre de domaines délégués par l'AFNIC," www.nic.fr/statistiques/afnic/afnic-repart.html [accessed March 13, 2003], in February 2002 there were 164,000 registered domain names under France's .fr. Despite having four times the population and a much larger economy than Chile, France had only twice the number of registered country code domain names.

16. For the current regulations for .cl, see "NIC Chile: Registro de Nombres del Dominio CL," NIC Chile, www.nic.cl/reglamentacion.html [accessed March 13, 2003].

17. For up-to-date .cl statistics, see NIC Chile at www.nic.cl/cgi-bin/Estadisticas/asignaciones [accessed March 13, 2003].

18. "Estadisticas NIC Chile," NIC Chile, www.nic.cl/stat.html [accessed March 13, 2003].

19. "Tarifas de Registro de Nombres de Dominio," NIC Chile, www.nic.cl/estudios/tarifas-cctlds [accessed March 13, 2003].

20. There have been other newsworthy conflicts over the rights to register domain names of cities and countries; see, for example, the dispute over Barcelona.com at http://ilectric.com/browse/web/Computers/Internet/Domain_Names/Disputed_Domain_Names/barcelona.com [accessed March 13, 2003]; see also the SouthAfrica.com dispute at www.itweb.co.za/sections/internet/2000/0011021213.asp [accessed March 13, 2003]; see also *Puerto Rico Tourism Company v. Virtual Countries, Inc.*, WIPO UDRP decision, April 14, 2003, at http://arbiter.wipo.int/domains/decisions/html/2002/d2002-1129.html [accessed May 18, 2003].

21. See "Denuncian a cyberocupas en registros de sitios web," Navarro.cl, September 4, 2000, www.navarro.cl/noticias/2000/septiembre/noticia016-4-9-2000.htm [accessed March 13, 2003]; see also Press Release, NIC Chile, September 6, 2000, www.nic.cl/anuncios/2000-09-06.html [accessed March 13, 2003].

~

CHAPTER FOUR

India's .IN: Underused and Underappreciated

Tushar A. Gandhi

It may come as a surprise to learn that in India, a nation of more than one billion people and a strong technology industry, there are fewer than 6,000 Internet websites ending with the Indian country code .in. Yet that is the case. Instead of concentrating sites within their country code top-level domain name space, as Chileans, for example, have done, Indian webmasters have largely abandoned their national code in favor of generic domain endings like .com.

Tushar A. Gandhi, the great-grandson of Mahatma Gandhi, argues that in doing so the Indian people have also abandoned their national pride. He shows this neglect through the social and bureaucratic hurdles he has faced in his attempts to build an Indian national identity on the Internet.

When I launched the Mahatma on the World Wide Web Project, India's first electronic archive dedicated to the life of the Mahatma Mohandas K. Gandhi in October 1997, I made conscious decisions not only about the content and design of the site but also about its Internet address.[1] Because the site deals with very specific Indian history, I was determined to connect the site to .in, the Indian country code top-level domain (ccTLD). A lot of friends told me not to insist on using the .in ccTLD, but I sought to have a ".org.in" domain to signify that the site was both not for profit and from India. I received comments like, "Who cares about .in?" "What difference does it make which country it comes from?" and "Why have three more key strokes?" It was not .in but rather .com that was the king of the Internet; it was .com that was the premier online address. Perhaps there was no place for national identity and pride in cyberspace.

During the .com boom of the 1990s, many people approached me and asked why I did not use the popular .com domain for the site. My response was that .com did not seem the appropriate choice for a free-reference website dedicated to the Mahatma, Mohandas K. Gandhi. To me, .com signifies being related to commerce and business, and my website was not a business site. Even in the United States I had noticed that government departments use .gov, universities use .edu, and voluntary organizations use .org. Apart from providing separate online identities, domain name endings also provide online visitors with information about the kind of website they are visiting. This connection is both logical and helpful.

Was the Internet confined only to .com? I quickly realized that most people did not recognize that .com was intended to be the top-level domain (TLD) for commercial entities and to be on an equal footing with all the other TLDs. Since .com had become the most famous Internet address ending, most people, and certainly most Indian people, decided that .com was more than an Internet address—it *was* the Internet. The distinctions between the various TLDs were lost in the clamor of the .com rush.[2]

Indians as a people have always accepted foreign endorsed ideologies and technologies over those that are homegrown. Even Mahatma Gandhi had to prove his mettle in South Africa before he was accepted as a leader in India. Similarly, the "Imported" label is highly sought after in India.[3] It is ironic that just over fifty-five years ago, we managed to successfully overthrow a colonial power by economically crippling it with a boycott of foreign goods.

On the Indian job front, a person with a foreign degree or foreign work experience is almost always preferred to those educated in India. Meanwhile, there is a global demand for people who have graduated from our Indian Institute of Technology and Indian Institute of Management.[4] This is one reason there has been a mass exodus of engineers and managers to foreign shores.

We have an institution of arranged marriages whereby the boy and girl are brought together by parents and relatives; even in arranged marriages, a foreign returned groom is preferred. Of course, a foreign settled groom is the prime catch.[5] It is not surprising that .com, which represented both the United States and the anonymity of the Internet, garnered more interest than .co.in.

Another reason for the popularity of .com over .co.in is a certain feeling of inferiority that we as an enslaved nation inherited from our forefathers. Immediately after independence, the fledgling Indian manufacturing industry acquired the reputation of producing substandard goods; it took a long time and a lot of effort on the part of Indian manufacturers to break into the markets of Europe and the United States.[6]

Many times finished goods were exported to countries that would affix a local "Made in" stamp on the Indian goods instead of "Made in India." This practice soon became acceptable to the developed world.[7] As a result, many people began to feel that those who knew that a product originated in India would be biased toward it and would brand it as inferior.[8] To economically protect their interests, many people continued to hide the fact that their products were from India.

Even in India, a common first reaction to a very well made object was, "Must be imported."[9] During the 1970s, although much of the denim cloth used by jeans manufacturers like Levi Strauss, Wrangler, and Lee was produced in Indian mills, the sale of Indian-made jeans was abysmally low.[10] To be considered "hip," one had to flaunt the imported label. I have seen this attitude rub off on the Internet; thus, for all our talk of nationalism and patriotism, we run after .com.

In addition to the psychological reasons, there are also more practical reasons Indian people preferred .com. A lot of the early Indiacentric material on the Internet was published by nonresident Indians who lived in the United States. For them, it was natural to register their sites with the .com extension. During the stampede for domain name registrations, I remember reading that Indians had registered the highest number of domains, all under .com. When these domains actually became websites, they did not bother to research or register the .co.in domains.

There are many examples of Indian people and organizations that should have naturally opted for a website in the .in name space but instead have registered their domains under generic TLDs. For example, neither the Bharatiya Janata Party (the nationalist Indian political party) nor the Indian National Congress (the party that won freedom for India and spearheaded Mahatma Gandhi's campaign of "boycott of foreign goods") has a website ending in .in.[11] Perhaps the most surprising example is that of the ultra-right-wing Hindu nationalist organization RSS (Rashtrya Svayamsevak Sangh),[12] an organization that crusades against foreign companies "invading" India and styles itself as the protector of Indian culture and the custodian of Indian national pride. Certainly, if there ever was an appropriate use for the .org.in domain, it would be for the RSS, but, in asking what difference it makes, they demonstrate that they are not at all sensitive to the issue.

I became an advocate for the use and promotion of the .in ccTLD because I saw the use of the ending as a way to let Internet users know that a website or even an e-mail was from India; without being chauvinistic, it was a matter of national pride. I strongly feel that India has a lot of content that would gain credibility by being classified as coming from India. A website dealing with yoga or Ayurveda (an ancient Indian system of herbal medicine and surgery) would gain more credibility if it used a .co.in, .info.in, or org.in domain name instead of .com.

India has gained for itself a premier position in the information technology world. Silicon Valley, the heart of information technology today, runs on the intellect and business acumen of Indian expatriates. The India label is no longer to be hidden from the world. To me, it is a matter of pride to announce to the world that I am an Indian and that the messages I send or the information I host on the Internet comes to the world from India. What can be a more subtle advertisement for India than the .in ccTLD?

My great-grandfather, Mahatma Gandhi, launched the movement of boycotting foreign goods, then largely British goods, not only to cripple the British industry and economy but also to instill a feeling of pride in Indians when they used Indian-made goods. They would do so not out of necessity but out of pride. As an Internet activist, I feel that when I sign an international petition with my e-mail address tushar@mahatma.org.in, at least Internet-savvy people will realize that this petitioner comes from India. Thus, what would be recognized is not only me as an individual but also my country as a part of me.

I once got into an argument with a very avid young Internet enthusiast who saw the Internet as a borderless, classless space; he believed that people like me were fragmenting the space by interposing geographical boundaries. His opinion was that I was corrupting the ideal of a faceless Internet by putting nationalist labels on it and by insisting on country-specific domain names. While he was genuinely angered by my campaign, I believe he had ignored the fact that I was not advocating a compulsory use of the .in ccTLD in India. It was my goal to create awareness about the availability of .in because the name alone would serve to broadcast to the world that the site was Indian. While my pursuits may have been nationalistic, they were not an attempt to divide. Still, the problems in promoting the use of the .in TLD are manifold.

What the young man failed to see was that the use of the .in ccTLD was not imposing national borders on the Internet. We cannot wish away the geographical borders that divide the world. No matter how much we wish to keep the virtual world free of identity tags, human beings, by nature, are individualistic and territorial. That is exactly why we use individualized e-mail addresses and descriptive domain names instead of merely random combinations of letters and numbers. If we are going to allow for individuality in the naming of e-mail addresses and domain names, why not go a step further and specify the geographical location by also using the unique ccTLD?

The argument that a ccTLD confines one to a narrow geographical location does not hold water. While registering an e-mail address at yahoo.com, I once mistakenly selected the United Kingdom as my country of domicile. Without asking me to furnish a real-world address in the United Kingdom, Yahoo! gave me an e-mail address that ended in "@yahoo.co.uk." The argument that requiring country-specific TLDs would fragment the Internet into regionalism, class divisions, and, in the case of India, caste barriers fails to explain the apathy of the Indian people toward the use of the .in ccTLD. The young man who was angered by my lobbying for the use of .in did not recognize that I was advocating a voluntary use of the .in ccTLD.

When the Internet became popular in India, it was only the generic top-level domains that were available. Based on their prevalence, as the Indian people became familiar with the Internet, they immediately got used to .com, .org, and .edu. India began to allow registrations in the .in name space in 1995. That is when the Internet really became accessible to the Indian citizens living in the cities.[13] At that time, there were 1.7 million Indian .com domains and only 645 .in domains.[14]

The first registrar of .in domain names was the National Centre for Software Technology (NCST; now known as C-DAC), a governmental scientific research and development institution.[15] The Internet Management Group has since been formed by the Indian government to oversee the registration activities under .in. This group consists of members from the state-owned Bharat Sanchar Nigam Limited, the Ministry of Communications and Information Technology of India, the formerly government-owned Videsh Sanchar Nigam Limited (VSNL; now privatized), and the NCST.

The first two private domain names registered with NCST were mafatlal.co.in and mg.co.in by businessmen Miheer Mafatlal and Kanakasabapathy Pandyan, respectively. Both of these men were my advisers when I set up the Gandhi eArchive. Mafatlal was the first person in India to have a personal leased line, a dedicated private line that is used primarily to link two remote networks; the others had dial-up access to the Internet. In the early days of the Internet in India, having a 640-kbps leased line of your own was a very expensive proposition that not many Indians could afford. Mafatlal was also one of the first to offer web hosting on his web server in the days when India had only one Internet Service Provider (ISP), the then-government-owned VSNL. Pandyan was chief executive officer of Micro Giga Infotech Private Limited, an information technology company owned by Mafatlal.

Since 1995, there have been only 5,465 .in registrations.[16] The reasons for such a low registration rate are both cultural and technological. Whereas in some TLD name spaces registrants have an opportunity to register directly under the TLD (for example, amazon.com or emmys.tv), other TLDs are more strictly divided into second-level domains. Within the .in name space, only ISPs can register their name directly under .in.[17] All others must register under a second-level domain that is determined by the type of site proposed. With 3,604 registrations, the most popular .in domain ending is .co.in, which is reserved for registered companies, banks, and those with trademarks.[18] Individuals may register sites under .ind.in.[19]

There are only six people who have overcome the tight restrictions and chosen to register a .ind.in domain; one is writing this chapter.[20] When I decided to register tushargandhi.ind.in, the domain was available. I sent in a request for the domain to be registered in my favor. I was surprised when I was told that, as a policy, any domain registered under .ind.in needed to have at least two numbers suffixed at the end of the name. This policy was an attempt to afford everyone a right to his or her name. If, for example, I registered tushargandhi.ind.in and another person named Tushar Gandhi wanted the same domain name, he would not get it. Because of this, the NCST and the Internet Management Group have decided that everyone seeking to register under the .ind.in domain must also include a number after his or her name because then the possibility for two identical addresses is much lower.

One of the advantages of the very strict rules governing the registration of a domain name under .in is that the stringent scrutiny has almost nullified incidents of cybersquatting, a practice where someone registers another's trademark as a domain name with the hope of selling it to the rightful owner at a profit. The problem is that while cybersquatting has been curbed, so too has lawful domain name registration.

While safeguards can sometimes be useful, they can also be too burdensome.[21] This is one such case. The registration should be on a first-come, first-served basis and require proper verification to determine whether the registrant has a bona fide use for the domain. Even though I was first and did not mind the longer address ending, I still could not get the tushargandhi.ind.in domain; I was forced to register tushargandhi01.ind.in.[22] The reasons there are so few domains registered under ind.in also contribute to the underutilization of the .in ccTLD as a whole.

As is often the case in India, there is a large bureaucracy that historically takes its time to do anything. The misfortune of India has been that its government is also an industrialist. The government of India is a big player in various industries through the large public sector undertakings in steel, oil, transportation, and even hospitality. This mentality has carried forward into the communications industry, especially the telecommunications (telecom) industry. Until very recently, telecom was a government monopoly.

The telephone network of India and the international communications were owned and managed by the government of India through the Ministry of Communications. As a result, there was a monopoly in the telecom sector controlled by the government. The domination soon extended to Internet services, which were also monopolized by the government with only one ISP: VSNL. It is only in the past two years that private companies have been allowed to own and manage their own international Internet connections.

It is probably little surprise that the registering of .in domain names was also under the authority of a government monopoly. This was one of the biggest stumbling blocks in promoting the .in ccTLD. While one could register a .com domain name online with nothing more than an ability to pay the fees as the registration criteria, registering a .in domain took at least forty-eight hours (if you were lucky), and you still had to furnish physical proof of your eligibility to use the name.

Registrants of .co.in and .edu.in domains had to display their company and Ministry of Education registration certificates. If that was not burdensome enough, the NCST required proof of an arrangement with an ISP and web-hosting service that would give you an IP (Internet Protocol) address, and the registration fees had to be paid by a bank draft, which required a trip to the bank. It was only after all these conditions were fulfilled that one could receive a domain name ending in .in. This was and continues to be a great hindrance in promoting the use of .in.

Even those who have a registrar's certificate must choose their domain names carefully; no generic names, like tea.co.in or diamond.co.in, are allowed. The fear in this case is of creating an unfair monopoly based on possible sales of the next level: fourth-level domain names. The fear is that one would register tea.co.in, for example, and also varieties of tea so that there would be a spate of orangepeko.tea.co.in, darjeeling.tea.co.in, and assam.tea.co.in, and things would get out of hand. There is also a commercial interest on the part of big tea companies that would object when someone used the .tea.co.in domain because it could harm their brands. This desire to prevent monopolies and restrictive trade practices is also reflected in non-Internet regulations, such as requiring businesses and charities to register with a commissioner.

While the regulations involving domain name registrations caused many Indian people to flee from .in, it is arguably the rules governing the technology that caused the most problems. From the 1995 introduction of .in until 2001, Indian users were deterred from registering sites under .in because they had to host their website on Indian soil, and there was only one ISP to choose from: VSNL. In those days, VSNL's rates were exorbitant, often running into several thousands of dollars per year.

Initially with VSNL, it cost 15,000 Indian rupees (U.S.$320) for a 500-hour account; while this was expensive, hosting a site with VSNL was even more expensive. Although located physically around the world, cheaper and less complicated web-hosting services in the United States managed to compete with India's VSNL.

Whenever arguments were made to allow private players into the ISP industry, the government would first exhaust other arguments and then rely on the necessity of national security. Similar tactics were used during the debates to allow Indians access to satellite phones.

The Defence Ministry has objected to the use of satellite phones, arguing that if they are made available in India, terrorists and antinational elements will use them to freely communicate with their benefactors and sponsors abroad, and the Indian security agencies will not be able to monitor them. While seemingly valid, the ground reality is that those very same terrorist organizations use satellite phones in India that were purchased and activated abroad. As long as their bills are paid in a foreign country, their satellite phones work, and the Indian security agencies can do nothing. As a result, it is only the legitimate users of satellite phones who are denied access by this policy.

Things have begun to change, however. Just as India has tried to cut red tape and tariffs and tear down socialist-era disincentives to foreign business, the rules governing .in have been relaxed.[23] Unfortunately, apathy to the .in ccTLD has grown; unless there is a well-orchestrated campaign to promote .in, Indians will not be sensitized to the importance of using the code.

Since 2001, NCST has allowed .in websites to be hosted anywhere. A majority of the sites are still hosted abroad, but now there are well-equipped private sector web-hosting facilities in India. The nation now has almost 200 ISPs offering Internet connectivity. Unfortunately, the .in registration process is still conducted by the Ministry of Communications and Information Technology through its appointee the NCST. I cannot fathom why the government does not allow the Indian ISPs and hosting companies to register .in domain names.

While there used to be no registration fee for a .in domain name, the current fees are still quite reasonable. At about half the price of .com domains, .in domains cost 1,500 rupees (U.S.$31.95) for a two-year registration. Even so, while NCST publishes the number of domains registered under each of the various second-level domains, it is unknown how many of the 5,465 are active; the result is that there are very few .in domains on the Internet.

Indians are by nature a bargain hunting people. Their shopping style is to haggle over the price. No matter how desperate they are to buy something, they will not be satisfied until they bargain with the seller and get the price reduced, if even by a fraction. Patients have been known to ask doctors for a discount in their fees before agreeing to treatment or surgery. If the .in registration monopoly were shattered, competition would drive the price down even farther, and the consumers would benefit. The difficulties faced by people attempting to register with NCST are partly to blame, but largely the cause of the low registration rate is the herd mentality of a nation believing that the Internet is confined to .com.

I had written to former Minister for Information Technology Pramod Mahajan with suggestions for enticing the Indian people to use the .in ccTLD. I proposed the more obvious lessening of paperwork. I recommended having more than one registrar for .in domains and offering online registration instead of requiring hard-copy registration to make it simpler, faster, and more user friendly. I encouraged him to make registration in certain second-level domains, like .gov.in and .edu.in free, to encourage Indian government departments and educational institutions to use .in addresses. Government departments and educational institutions are always short of funds and would never pay for a domain name. I also suggested that he make it compulsory for all government departments to use .in addresses to show support for the domain.

Finally, I asked Mahajan to promote the use of .in on the Swadeshi ("homegrown") nationalistic platform. Swadeshi was the movement of boycotting foreign goods started by Mahatma Gandhi during our freedom movement; it is, to this day, a very nationalistic slogan and philosophy. The other reason is that the BJP, the political arm of the Rashtrya Svayamsevak Sangh, an ultranationalist right-wing Hindu organization, is in power in India. One of its electoral platforms is the promotion of Swadeshi. One of the BJP's sister organizations is the Swadeshi Jagran Manch, which is a vocal promoter of domestic products and industries.

In response to my letter, I was contacted by a secretary from the ministry who profusely thanked me for my very "intelligent" input and assured me that they would use my suggestions while framing the policy and procedures for popularizing the use of .in. This was in January 2002; I have yet to see any significant change.

These are considered nonessential issues. They are revived only when a bureaucrat wants to divert attention from other issues or when the minister is accused of nonperformance. Unfortunately, as I write this chapter, Mahajan has been fired from the cabinet of the central government of India.

There is a new minister in charge of information technology and communications; Arun Shouri will have his own priorities. I now prepare to petition this minister and hope that he will take it up as his own cause.

In December 2002, NCST and several other research societies merged to form the Centre for Development of Advanced Computing (C-DAC). It is

NCST, redesignated as C-DAC, that is the authority for managing .in. Yet, when visiting the C-DAC website at www.cdac.org.in, the first page says, "http://www.cdacindia.com."[24]

In September 2001, my struggle to popularize the .in ccTLD was reported in *Wired News*.[25] After the article was published, the letters I received reminded me that there are a variety of reasons to promote the use of ccTLDs; mine is to inform.

For me, the main reason for using the .in is national pride. Since it would also inform the recipient that I am not trying to hide under a veil of anonymity, I am clearly acknowledging my geographical location. When the World Wide Web came into existence, it was essential for those who wanted to be identified with their country, on the borderless Internet, to be able to do so with a country-specific extension to the domain name. Why not use it?

Although .com may be king in cyberspace, for me, .in is a matter of pride and belonging.

Notes

1. See The Official Mahatma Gandhi eArchive at www.mahatma.org.in [accessed January 21, 2003].

2. For more information about the top-level domains and their foundational structure, see Jon Postel, "Domain Name System Structure and Delegation" (Network Working Group, Request for Comments No. 1591), March 1994, www.rfc-editor. org/rfc/rfc1591.txt [accessed March 13, 2003].

3. See, for example, Mamatha Maben, "The Positives and the Value of Wright," Thatscricket.com, June 9, 2001, www.thatscricket.com/columnists/mamatha/ 090601india.html [accessed March 17, 2003]; see also "Sensual Notes," *Deccan Herald*, January 25, 2003, www.deccanherald.com/deccanherald/jan25/liv6.asp [accessed March 17, 2003].

4. Radhakrishna Rao, "India's Silicon Valley: A Software Mecca," *India Perspectives*, December 1997, www.meadev.nic.in/perspec/dec97/SiliconValley.htm [accessed March 20, 2003].

5. See, for example, "Indian Weddings," A-Z Tours International, www. a-ztours.com/indiaweddings.htm [accessed March 20, 2003], which notes, "The main determining factor [of a dowry amount] is the level of education and social standing of the young man: a dowry of at least US $20,000 would be expected from the family of a young woman hoping to marry a graduate of a foreign university, a Doctor or other highly paid professional"; see also "Meet the Kanya!" Dharwad.com, www.dharwad.com/nimmaputa/meet_the_kanya.html [accessed March 20, 2003], which says, "It's no exaggeration if I say the big corporate names' IPOs [initial public offerings] have not only affected stock trading but also affected the small middle class homes of Dharwad. A dream of getting a son-in-law who works for a software company and is a potential 'NRI' [nonresident Indian]."

6. See, for example, S. Gurumurthy, "Making India an Economic Super Power," *The Tribune*, August 15, 1998, www.tribuneindia.com/50yrs/final.htm [accessed March 13, 2003].

7. See N. Ramakrishnan, "Made in India Label for Manufacturing Needs Push," *The Hindu Business Line*, November 24, 2002, www.blonnet.com/bline/2002/11/25/stories/2002112500700500.htm [accessed March 20, 2003]; see more generally, Amanullah Bashar, "Made in Pakistan," *Pakistan Economist*, August 15, 1999, www.pakistaneconomist.com/issue1999/issue32/cover.htm [accessed March 20, 2003].

8. See Kaushik Basu, "The Enigma of Advertising," *India Today*, September 11, 1999, http://people.cornell.edu/pages/kb40/9.13.99.pdf [accessed March 20, 2003].

9. See, for example, Anamika Ahluwalia, "Made in Italy," Rediff.com, April 3, 1997, www.rediff.com/style/apr/03gabba.htm [accessed March 20, 2003].

10. See, for example, Miriam Jordan, "Dungarees Fit Delhi Just Fine," *Christian Science Monitor*, November 21, 1997.

11. See Bharatiya Janata Party at www.bjp.org [accessed March 13, 2003], and Indian National Congress at www.indiancongress.org [accessed March 13, 2003].

12. See RSS at www.rss.org [accessed March 13, 2003].

13. The top ten cities contribute 60 percent of the total Internet penetration in India; see "Who Uses the Internet in India?" Bangalorenet.com, www.bangalorenet.com/internetindia [accessed February 18, 2003]. It was only in the late 1980s that the vast rural population was connected with telephone lines.

14. "Host Distribution by Top-Level Domain Name," Internet Software Consortium, July 1995, www.isc.org/ds/WWW-9507/dist-byname.html [accessed January 21, 2003].

15. See NCST at www.ncst.ernet.in [accessed January 21, 2003].

16. "Indian Domain Name Registration," NCST, May 5, 2003, http://domain.ncst.ernet.in/statistics.php [accessed May 18, 2003].

17. See, for example, Education and Research Network India (ERNET) at www.ernet.in [accessed January 21, 2003].

18. See, for example, National Geographic Channel India at www.nationalgeographic.co.in [accessed March 13, 2003], Yahoo! India at www.yahoo.co.in [accessed March 13, 2003], and Sony India at www.sonyindia.co.in [accessed March 13, 2003].

19. For the full list of second-level .in TLDs and their registration requirements, see "Indian Domain Name Registration: General Terms and Conditions," NCST, http://domain.ncst.ernet.in/termsandconditions.php [accessed January 21, 2003].

20. "Status on the Number of Domains Registered under .IN Domain," NCST, May 5, 2003, http://hdomain.ncst.ernet.in/statistics.php [accessed January 21, 2003].

21. For the complete registration requirements, see, for example, "Indian Domain Name Registration: General Terms and Conditions," NCST, http://domain.ncst.ernet.in/termsandconditions.php [accessed January 21, 2003], or "Domain FAQs," Internet Users Community of India, www.iucimumbai.org.in/domain.html [accessed January 21, 2003].

22. Although I have registered the domain tushargandhi01.ind.in, I must confess that I have still not gotten around to creating my website. At the moment, I can be

classified as a good-faith cybersquatter—sitting on the domain tushargandhi01.ind. in. I must make clear, though, that I have no intention of selling the domain name. One fine day, I will create my site and activate the URL.

23. See, for example, Indira A. R. Lakshmanan, "Clinton Ends India Trip with Focus on High Tech," *Boston Globe*, March 25, 2000; see also Kripa Raman, "Indian Cos Missing Out on the 'In' Thing," *The Hindu Business Line*, May 29, 2000, www.thehindubusinessline.com/businessline/2000/05/31/stories/15313911.htm [accessed February 18, 2003].

24. See C-DAC at www.cdac.org.in [accessed May 22, 2003].

25. See Manu Joseph, "Young Gandhi's Crusade Is Dot-In," *Wired News*, September 3, 2001, www.wired.com/news/culture/0,1284,46339,00.html [accessed January 21, 2003].

~

CHAPTER FIVE

Malaysia's .MY: Globalization and Domain Identification among Malaysian Students

Toby E. Huff

It is not only Indians who shy away from their national codes. In fact, low Internet development and internationalist visions create little use for many Muslim nation country code top-level domains (ccTLDs).

For many years, sociology and anthropology professor Toby E. Huff has studied the intersection of technology and culture. Here he presents new research that shows that Malaysian university students prefer the international identities afforded to them by generic domain names to national identities that are gained by using Malaysia's ccTLD, .my.

The design of the World Wide Web in the mind of its creator, Tim Berners-Lee, was intentionally universal in scope. His vision called for the creation of a universal information network that would allow all network users to access and post documents of all kinds from any place on the planet.[1] Consequently, when Internet Service Providers (ISPs) began creating e-mail services in the 1990s, they entered a communications environment that was global in scope. Needless to say, the creation of this universal communications system inescapably advanced the process of globalization and the global connectedness of the peoples of the world.

Although we take this globalized attitude for granted, we should not overlook the fact that this universal design was indeed a radical idea. When Berners-Lee proposed his "Universal Resource Identifier" (URI), the generic term for all types of names and addresses that refer to objects on the World

Wide Web, American engineers and Internet designers at a 1992 Boston meeting said he was "arrogant" to imagine such a universal system. They seemed to want a more limited Internet design than what Berners-Lee envisioned.[2]

We should not lose sight of the fact that historically the globe has been divided by ethnic, linguistic, religious, and civilizational divisions. Although these divisions should not be exaggerated, as we will see shortly, the fact is that some ethnic and religious groups view themselves as denizens of a non-Western cultural and linguistic space.

For example, when Professor Elizabeth Fernea embarked on her journey in search of "Islamic feminism" to a half dozen or so Muslim countries in the Middle East and North Africa (MENA) in the mid-1990s, she repeatedly heard respondents say that they did not want to be called "feminists," even though their political and social activities clearly suggested such a label. Many women responded that they wanted "their own term," not a Western term.[3]

Likewise, during my own visits to the MENA, I often heard wistful expressions of a desire to resurrect a new "Arab empire," an empire based on the presumed authenticity and moral superiority of the Islamic faith. Deeply rooted in such expressions was the assumption that the only solid basis for a new society and civilization was the moral grounding that Islam provided. To be sure, my hosts in Syria, for example, were exceedingly generous and friendly toward me and almost infinitely curious about Western attitudes and mores. Nevertheless, there was an underlying presumption that the "West," above all the United States, was undergoing moral decay that was most evident in the apparently collapsing American family. In 2000, Syria did not have a single ISP, though this was partly due to import restrictions.

In other parts of the world, in Southeast Asia, for example, one can also point to claims of "otherness," as in the once-intense debate over "Asian values" put forth by political leaders such as Lee Kuan Yew of Singapore.[4] He insisted that the unrestrained liberal democracy of the West—coupled with broad human rights, manifested in the unruly posting of everyone's opinion in the public domain and the celebration of individualism—ran counter to such Asian values as restraint, orderly, controlled public discourse, and the wide embrace of family and community. In his view, only a rare, highly trained and disciplined elite is capable of properly running Singapore or any other self-respecting society.

In short, in Southeast Asia the worries about Western decadence are still present, though there is no underlying assumption of an emerging "Asian," much less Muslim, civilization.[5] Indeed, all such discussions about the putative unity of Asia (as in ASEAN, the Association of Southeast Asian Nations) quickly reveal the divisions that exist.

Malaysia is the most Internet-developed country in the Muslim world, apart from the tiny but oil-rich United Arab Emirates.[6] Malaysia is a Muslim majority country of 22.6 million people located in Southeast Asia. The Muslim Malays make up about 58 percent of the population, with 25 percent ethnic Chinese, 8 percent Indians, and 10 percent others. Malaysia's literacy rate of 84 percent is high by world standards and much higher than Muslim countries generally. The Malay Peninsula, extending south from Thailand, is bordered on the south by the Straits of Malacca and on the north by the South China Sea. Singapore, the separated city-state of mainly ethnic Chinese, lies at the tip of the peninsula. Two additional provinces of Malaysia, Sarawak and Sabah, lie on the northern border of the island of Borneo.

Malaysia was a British colony from the middle of the nineteenth century until 1957, when it gained its independence. Administratively, Malaysia has thirteen states and two federal territories and enjoys a parliamentary form of government. Malaysia has many natural resources, including tin, and rich agricultural land, as well as oil and natural gas. It attempts to maintain a balanced economy with 28 percent of the labor force in local trade and tourism, 27 percent in manufacturing, and 16 percent in agriculture, forestry, and fisheries. Services, government, and construction account for about 10 percent each.[7]

In the early 1990s, the leadership of Malaysia, especially Prime Minister Mahathir Mohamad, began to recognize that the Internet was the major connection to the new "information age" and the "knowledge" economy. He and his advisers also theorized that the Internet—properly developed and synchronized with other aspects of the Malaysian economic infrastructure— could serve as a new engine of economic growth.[8] This led to the launching of a very ambitious project to construct an Internet-based infrastructure that was called a "multimedia supercorridor" (MSC). This project was launched in 1996 and resulted in the construction of an elaborate fiber-optic Internet core running through what the leadership hopes will be the central economic backbone of the country. By 1999, the MSC was up and running, with many new ambitious adjuncts to the system in the planning and development stage.[9] All these efforts were tied to the equally ambitious plan to make Malaysia a fully "developed" country by 2020. Furthermore, it is evident that the leadership of Malaysia has very adroitly stimulated and encouraged strong nationalistic sentiments among Malaysians. This is evident on the radio and in television spots during which nationalistic songs, celebrations, and other rituals are repeatedly performed.

It is instructive to point out that the registration of country code top-level domains (ccTLDs) began universally in 1985; it was only two years later, in 1987, that Malaysia was delegated .my, the ccTLD for Malaysia.

Thus, Malaysia was one of only nineteen countries, and the first Muslim country, that had been delegated a ccTLD by 1987.[10]

The delegation of authority went to MIMOS Berhad, a mission-oriented research-and-development government corporation that set up an internal division, namely, the Malaysian Network Information Centre (MYNIC), to register domain names.[11] It should be noted that MIMOS (the Malaysian Institute of Microelectronic Systems) was the original administrative unit that masterminded and launched Malaysia's multimedia supercorridor mentioned previously.

Registrations for .my domain names are restricted to government registered and certified organizations operating in Malaysia, which means that individuals cannot register domain names under .my. This policy seems to reflect the greater inclination of Asian governments to work through groups rather than individuals. In addition, it is a useful sorting mechanism for identifying reputable public or commercial agents. Beyond that, the governments of developing countries like Malaysia are keen to regulate all foreign direct investment and to monitor which multinational or other non-Malaysian companies become active in the Malaysian economy.

The .my name space supports domain name registrations under six second-level domains that were drafted to mirror the generic top-level domains (gTLDs).

As a result, those seeking to register domain names must choose between the .com.my, .org.my, .mil.my, .edu.my, .net.my, and .gov.my suffixes. The popularity of the endings mirrors the popularity of the gTLDs; more than 90 percent of the 36,696 .my domain names end in .com.my,[12] which reflects the international pattern of domain name registrations. When registering specific domain names, registrants are forbidden to register words "in either English, or Bahasa Malaysia, that are sensitive to the main religions in Malaysia such as 'Islam,' 'Buddha,' 'Hindu,' 'Christianity.'"[13] Registrants also must not register geographic terms and words that "by themselves, or as part of a label, are obscene, scandalous, indecent, offensive, or contrary to Malaysian public norms."[14] These restrictions serve to prevent any interreligious or interethnic conflict and above all to protect Islam from any kind of slander or defamation, real or imagined. This policy sensibly extends such protection to all the major active religious communities in Malaysia. Such restrictions are common in Muslim countries.

Finally, domain name registrants must not register names containing the words "bank" or "finance company" (or any derivative of the words in any language) unless they have received the written consent of the minister of finance. These restrictions appear to reflect the much closer monitoring of bank and finance company creation in the country. There is a great sensitivity among certain segments of the Malaysian elite about maintaining control of its banking system and especially forestalling takeovers by multinational conglomerates. This sentiment prevails despite the recognition in some official circles that Malaysian banks are inefficient and ought to eliminate thousands of redundant workers.

In this context, it is useful to consider the various identities that Asians can assume in the process of becoming Internet users. The most obvious such identifier is the domain name built into the Internet structure through the top-level domain names. This means that Internet users have a choice as to whether they want to have an e-mail address with a country code identification, as in "name@UM.edu.my" (where "UM" stands for "University of Malaya" [an educational institution] and "my" stands for "Malaysia"), or an e-mail address with no such identifier, as in "name@Yahoo.com." The latter gives no indication of the user's national identity, place of residence, or server's location.

Given this background and the nationalistic orientation of contemporary Malaysia, it is instructive to examine the domain identifications of Malaysian young people, especially university students. To do that, I had a very short questionnaire administered to a small group of Malaysian students studying at the International Islamic University Malaysia (IIUM), located just outside the capital city of Kuala Lumpur.

Founded in 1983, the IIUM is a rather new university that has a somewhat special mission. As reflected in its name, the IIUM seeks to educate its students in a manner that preserves an Islamic tradition based on *tawhid*, that is, "unity" of spiritual and intellectual insights. This mission has also been presented as part of the "Islamization" of knowledge project, also begun in the early 1980s.[15] That term is exceedingly ambiguous as a practical matter, but the intent is to harmonize all knowledge with the underlying presuppositions of Islam. Even stating this prospect of alignment suggests that there is an ontological or metaphysical gap between the Islamic outlook and that of all others. Nevertheless, the program of instruction at the university is at once ambitious, international, and progressive. That is, in addition to teaching the "revealed sciences," especially Islamic law and the prophetic tradition, the IIUM teaches communication technology, economics, engineering, management sciences, law, and medicine. Furthermore, the primary language of instruction is English, something that was made possible by incorporating the university under a special "Company Act" law that permits a publicly funded institution to use a language other than Malay for instructional purposes. In general, the courses of instruction are standardized on the American model, and the leaders of the country expect students at the IIUM to perform well on the international level. It has just under

11,000 students, and these students seem to be a bit more liberal than their conservative faculty mentors. The University of Malaya, the older, larger, and more comprehensive university, has a more secular and probably more internationally well-known faculty but also teaches most courses in the Malay language.

One of the first surprises of the survey data is that the majority, 63 percent, of these students had e-mail accounts before they entered the university.[16] This seems very similar to the pattern of American university students, especially in nonelite schools, whose preuniversity e-mail ownership is probably closer to 90 percent. This result suggests both the middle-class status of the students and the wide availability of Internet access. Moreover, this group of students had an average of two e-mail accounts; some obviously have more than two accounts.

When asked how important it is for the IIUM students to have an e-mail account with a Malaysian identity, 42 percent said that it was "very important." Consequently, 58 percent responded by saying that it was only "slightly" or less important to have a Malaysian e-mail identity. When it came to describing their preferred e-mail account provider—a Malaysian ISP or an international provider—fully 72 percent chose an international provider. Despite the nationalistic guidance of the central government, these students prefer international Internet identities.

To ascertain the actual identities of these e-mail accounts, the respondents were asked to check off the various companies with whom they have accounts. The results of this question show overwhelmingly that the students prefer international rather than Malaysian service providers. The two top providers of e-mail accounts were Yahoo.com and Hotmail.com, but Yahoo! was the most popular by far, with about 30 percent more Yahoo! than Hotmail accounts. As noted, most students have more than one e-mail address. If we consider all these accounts, the percentage of the accounts that potentially would have Malaysian domain identifications (a .my extension) is about 6 percent; roughly 94 percent of all the accounts are international. Clearly, these students prefer international over Malaysian identities. It seems apparent that choosing an e-mail account provider does, in fact, amount to choosing an identity. This happens on many different levels, including in the United States, with the choice of a "cool" name, such as "YourDayintheSun," "fatcat," and so on, rather than one's own real name. A Malaysian academic pointed out to me that when he was conducting "official" business, he would use his academic account, complete with the university name and the .edu.my extension. On the other hand, if he were engaged in some kind of "political" discussion, he would use his Yahoo! or Hotmail account and would avoid using an account that provided a Malaysian identifier.

The reasons for such choices are indeed complex and varied, but they do include concerns about official surveillance. It is true, of course, that the Yahoo! and Hotmail accounts are free, but that does not seem to be a factor in these considerations, as the students would have to have some ISP to get onto the web in any event—unless they used only Internet cafés or possibly university accounts.

Conversations I have had with students at IIUM suggest that they are keen not to be seen as provincials, as culturally "backward." Thus, they seem eager to opt for an international identity. However, as in the previous example, there is a general concern in Malaysia about potential surveillance by governmental authorities in cases involving political dissent. The Malaysian government has enunciated an official policy of no censorship with regard to communication on the MSC, but Malaysians are skeptical about the boundaries of such putative safe zones. One could imagine a politically sensitive e-mail being found by authorities on the server at a university or other location; in the absence of well-established case law protecting such communications, there are reasons for Internet users to be skeptical about the security of their e-mail. While only a little more than a quarter of the students say they are "very worried" about being watched while on the Internet, about 30 percent are "slightly worried." This means that a full 58 percent of the students are either very or slightly worried about surveillance.

In general, the government appears to have honored its commitment not to censor communications flowing over the MSC. However, there was a recent case in which authorities did step in and seize what the government took to be politically offensive material. This occurred when an online newspaper, *Malaysiakini*, published a letter in early January 2003 in which a pseudonymous author drew an analogy between the "ethnic cleansing" carried out by Americans (European colonialists) with regard to Native Americans (dispossessed their land, put them on reservations, and so on) and the policies of the Malaysian government that grant privileges and economic advantages to the "Bumiputera," the so-called people of the land but construed as Malays.[17] Several days after the posting of the letter, the police arrived at the offices of *Malaysiakini*, demanding that all the computer files relating to the letter be turned over. The police then proceeded to remove many of the servers, including ones not containing the letter. This resulted in the temporary halting of publication by *Malaysiakini* until new servers were installed.[18] This case is very serious because it surely suggests not only that government officials are watching but also that they will take action to punish political speech that they deem offensive.

A prior incident occurred in December 2002, when the police arrested seven people who were accused of using e-mail to "spread rumors." In this case, there were rumors that terrorists had planted bombs in several shopping complexes in Kuala Lumpur. The letters were sent to the Australian High Commission. As far the Malaysian police were concerned, the claims were false and hence constituted dangerous information "that could disrupt public order." In this case, the arrests were made under the Internal Security Act.[19]

Apart from these concerns about political surveillance, perhaps there are issues of convenience related to these choices of international e-mail account providers. These have to do with the ubiquitous availability of account access when using Yahoo! and Hotmail accounts. Such accounts can be accessed from any point on the planet where there is an Internet-enabled computer. In addition, international ISPs are at least perceived to be more efficient, especially when compared to university servers that too often crash.

Nevertheless, given these and other considerations, it seems apparent that in addition to becoming more "international" and cosmopolitan by opening a Yahoo! or Hotmail account, users are greatly worried about political repercussions if they should engage in political discussions and have their true identities revealed. Discussions I have had with citizens of Middle Eastern or North African countries, such as Tunisia, suggest a similar aversion to revealing their identities through their e-mail account names. Moreover, other restrictions that are often built into the national communications networks, such as proxy servers, suggest that international e-mail accounts provide greater access to the unfettered web. That is, if a user can get logged on to a Yahoo! e-mail account located on a server outside his or her country, the probability that the e-mail message will be delivered is much greater than if the e-mail server were within the country because some countries install message-blocking software. But having a pseudonymous Yahoo! e-mail account does not protect one from ultimate personal identification by authorities. If security experts were to attempt to trace an e-mail message by someone using a pseudonym, it could be done whether the e-mail account were Yahoo! or some other account.

The World Wide Web was invented to create a universal information network, one in which users would be able to access as well as add to the existing stock of information. Even prior to that communications revolution, the development of the Internet under mainly American auspices in the 1980s resulted in the creation of a domain name system that incorporated both country code and generic top-level domain names. This was done as a simple matter of expediency to administer the burgeoning global spread of the Internet. In this way, the need for a manageable administrative structure reintroduced into the Internet world the divisions of country and nationality that came with the country code registrations starting in 1985.

Some observers might have supposed that this recidivist move would fracture the Internet, turning it into a congeries of nationalistic identities.

Indeed, that battle has not yet been won, as national entities continue, even now, to control access to the World Wide Web through proxy servers that monitor and block access to so-called sensitive sites. Not a few of these servers are programmed to block access to "forbidden" sites on the web, however futile such blocking will be in the long run. Moreover, the very low ranking of Muslim countries around the world on the scale of Internet development as measured by the number of Internet hosts per capita[20] reveals the very uneven levels of commitment to Internet access and development by national political and business elites.

Nevertheless, as the data in this study reveal, young aspiring Muslim university students in Malaysia are overwhelmingly committed to international and hence not national identities insofar as Internet communication is concerned. The responses indicate that fully 72 percent of these students at a major Islamic university in Malaysia are in favor of international Internet identities. The actual e-mail accounts used by these students indicate that by a margin of greater than ten to one, they select international e-mail account providers. Among these, Yahoo.com and Hotmail.com are the unquestioned leaders, with Yahoo! having a four-to-three advantage over Hotmail.

These results suggest that there is strong desire among these students not to be seen as culturally retarded. At the same time, there are issues of privacy and surveillance that may incline young Malaysians to opt for international identities so as not to be recognized immediately as a Malaysian political actor, but it seems likely that today's Internet users know that having a Yahoo! e-mail account does not protect them from security surveillance and that their personal identities can be discovered by security officials if the latter decide to investigate.

Apart from these issues of monitoring and surveillance—and Malaysia ought to be regarded as one of the most open and unrestricted countries in the Muslim world, as it is even more unfettered than Singapore—the existence of a variety of impediments controlling access to the Internet in developing countries is clearly restraining Internet development and with it many of the commercial opportunities that go with Internet development. Most obviously, it suggests that in addition to international identities, young people prefer content that is provided by international actors and knowledge creators. By erecting the various barriers that exist on the national level in many countries, it would seem that those national policies of restriction are inadvertently encouraging young people to seek international identities. From the point of view of global harmony and communication, this seems all to the good, except that, as mentioned, trust in Internet-related products with international identities will continue to crowd out local and national ones, thereby extending unwanted global domination from outside, usually read as Americanization.

Notes

1. Nothing I say here is intended to overlook the early history of the Internet, its development by the Advanced Research Projects Agency (ARPA) in the 1960s, its first public demonstration in 1972, and subsequent developments. Among the many sources of this history, see Janet Abbate, *Inventing the Internet* (Cambridge, Mass.: MIT Press, 1999), as well as Thomas P. Hughes, *Rescuing Prometheus* (New York: Pantheon, 1998), especially chapter 6.

2. See Tim Berners-Lee, *Weaving the Web: The Original Design and Ultimate Destiny of the World Wide Web* (New York: HarperCollins, 1999), 61. Berners-Lee's concept of a Universal Resource Identifier (URI) had to be changed to Uniform Resource Locator (URL).

3. Elizabeth Fernea, *In Search of Islamic Feminism: One Woman's Global Journey* (New York: Doubleday, 1998).

4. Daniel A. Bell, *East Meets West: Human Rights and Democracy in East Asia* (Princeton, N.J.: Princeton University Press, 2000).

5. After the Asian currency crisis of 1997–1998 and the decline of Japan, the short-lived enthusiasm for a "Pacific century" has gone underground.

6. Toby E. Huff, "Globalization and the Internet: Comparing the Middle Eastern and Malaysian Experiences," *Middle East Journal* 55, no. 3 (2001): 439–58, and "Malaysia's Multimedia Super Corridor and Its First Crisis of Confidence," *Asian Journal of Social Science* 30, no. 2 (2002): 248–70.

7. See Central Intelligence Agency, "Malaysia," *World Factbook*, February 13, 2003, www.cia.gov/cia/publications/factbook/geos/my.html [accessed March 13, 2003].

8. See references in note 6.

9. Huff, "Globalization and the Internet," 439–58.

10. "History of the Internet: ccTLDs in Chronological Order of Top Level Domain Creation at the Internic," www.wwtld.org/aboutcctld/history/wwtld1999/ccTLDs-by-date.html [accessed March 13, 2003], and Elisabeth Porteneuve, "Country Code Top Level Domain Names—ccTLD—History in the Making," www.afnog.org/ccTLD-history-in-the-making.htm [accessed March 13, 2003].

11. See the MYNIC home page at www.mynic.net [accessed March 13, 2003].

12. See "Statistics" from the MYNIC home page at www.mynic.net [accessed March 13, 2003].

13. See "Choosing a Domain Name," MYNIC, www.mynic.net.my/newhp/MYNIC-011_Choices.htm [accessed March 13, 2003].

14. See note 13.

15. For further discussion of this tortured subject, see Leif Stenberg, *The Islamization of Science: Four Muslim Positions Developing an Islamic Modernity* (Lund: Almqvist & Wiksell, 1996), and Toby E. Huff, "Can Scientific Knowledge Be Islamized?" *Social Epistemology* 10, no. 3/4 (1996): 305–16.

16. The discussion to follow is based on an analysis of a short questionnaire administered to a small sample of upper-class psychology majors ($n = 79$) at the International Islamic University Malaysia during the first week of January 2003. I thank

Professor Zafar Ansari of the IIUM for his generous assistance in administering the survey instrument. Since this is not a strictly random sample, no claim is made about its representativeness for all Malaysian students.

17. See "Similarities between 'New Americans' and Bumiputera," MalaysiaKini. com, January 9, 2003, at www.malaysiakini.com/letters/200301090033726.php [accessed March 5, 2003].

18. See, for example, "Malaysiakini Awaits the Return of Four Servers in Police Custody," Digital Freedom Network, February 4, 2003, www.dfn.org/news/malaysia/ servers.htm [accessed March 5, 2003].

19. See "Two Held over Terror Rumour," *The Courier-Mail*, www.couriermail. news.com.au/common/story_page/0,5936,5697392%255E15574,00.html [accessed March 5, 2003].

20. These statistics are published annually by the United Nations Human Development Program in its annual reports on human development; see *Human Development Report 2002: Deepening Democracy in a Fragmented World* (New York: Oxford University Press, 2002), table 11, or http://hdr.undp.org/reports/global/2002/en [accessed March 13, 2003].

CHAPTER SIX

~

Sweden's .SE: Reestablishing Itself as the Best Choice for All Swedes

Patrik Lindén

Just as many members of the Islamic world see .com as being more pro-gressive than their national country code domains, other societies also have relationships with domains other than their national codes. In Sweden, re-strictive domain registration policies have kept many Swedes from using the Swedish country code top-level domain, .se, and encouraged them to use other codes. The policies resulted in the dispersal of the Swedish population on the Internet.

Patrik Lindén, a communications officer at the Swedish Internet Infra-structure Foundation (IIS), the organization responsible for the managing of .se, discusses the exodus from .se and the efforts that have been taken to bring the Swedish people back to their national code.

Sweden is a technologically advanced nation. In 2001, two-thirds of the Swedish population had Internet access, and in 2003, Sweden was listed as the nation most conducive to Internet-based opportunities.[1] The country also ranks among the top, alongside the United States and the other Scan-dinavian countries, in surveys that measure the maturity of a nation's in-formation technology infrastructure.[2] As a result of the nation's high level of technological sophistication, the choice of an Internet top-level domain (TLD) has become a practical issue for a large portion of the population.

While by early 2003, .se, Sweden's country code top-level domain (ccTLD), had more than 100,000 registered domain names and a clear association with Sweden, it was far from being the only domain under which Swedes registered. The .se name space was filled primarily with companies and public sector bodies, but the .com and .nu domains also had prominent shares of the Swedish market.[3] This is due mainly to a history of strict .se registration policies. In an attempt to curb the exodus from .se, in April 2003, Sweden implemented drastic policy changes to further open .se to the entire Swedish population.

The history of .se goes back to 1986, when the .se domain was granted to the supervision of a Swedish computer scientist named Björn Eriksen. In 1983, Eriksen had received what was, in all likelihood, Sweden's first e-mail; this made him an ideal candidate to manage the domain. At the time of the delegation, Eriksen worked with the European Unix Network (EUnet), which was Europe's first computer network. As a precursor to the larger Internet, EUnet provided e-mail and newsgroup services for users in the Netherlands, Denmark, Sweden, and the United Kingdom. The EUnet used identifiers that were called "node names"; these addressing names were later converted to being what we now think of as domain names.

Enea, the information technology company where Björn Eriksen worked at the time, was the first .se domain name to be registered. Other early domain name holders for .se were the universities and colleges of technology in Stockholm, Lund, and Gothenburg and telecom company Ericsson. Still, barely 100 domain names were registered in the domain's first five years.[4] It was not until the beginning of the 1990s that interest in Sweden began to focus on information technology in general and on the Internet in particular.

Carl Bildt, Sweden's prime minister from 1991 to 1994, actively pursued information technology issues and brought the Internet, the World Wide Web, and e-mail to the attention of many Swedes. After leaving office, Bildt later worked with the Internet-governing body, Internet Corporation for Assigned Names and Numbers (ICANN).

The Swedish society's interest in the Internet became clear in 1994, when parliamentary elections were held in Sweden and many newspapers sought to obtain election results continuously via EUnet. This fusion of technology and the democratic process led to media attention that soon focused on other aspects of the Internet. The increased interest in the Internet was also reflected by an increase in domain name registrations.

Nearly twice as many .se domain names were registered during 1994 as during the entire period preceding it. Since 1995, the growth has been steady. More than 20,000 .se domain names were registered during 1996.[5]

While most Swedes know that .se is the Swedish TLD on the Internet, few of them know how the domain is organized or who governs it. The .se organization has kept a fairly low profile in Swedish life. Many people assume that it is a government authority; this type of system would mirror that of the telephone numbers under the Swedish country code, +46, for which the government is responsible. In fact, .se is administered by a non-profit organization, the Swedish Foundation for Internet Infrastructure (the II Foundation), which is known as II-stiftelsen in Sweden.[6]

In 1997, Björn Eriksen recognized that the sheer number of registrations meant that it was no longer possible for one person to administer the .se domain. On October 8, he delegated responsibility for the .se domain to the II Foundation. The delegation was later ratified by the Internet Assigned Numbers Authority, which at that time coordinated the administration of domain names at the global level. With this transfer, the act of registering the .se domain names changed from being a hobby reserved for enthusiasts to an activity with fiscal demands that required a more stable and formal organization.

The Swedish chapter of the international Internet Society, ISOC-SE, was behind the creation of the II Foundation; the board of directors was initially comprised of members of ISOC-SE, the Swedish Network Users' Society, the Swedish Internet Operators' Forum, and a trademark lawyer from the Confederation of Swedish Enterprise.

Today, the board has been expanded to include representatives appointed by the Swedish Federation of Trade, the Swedish Consumer Agency, the Swedish Information Processing Society, and the Swedish Bankers' Association. The aim behind the composition of the board is to guarantee technical expertise and representation from a broad spectrum of society and various user groups.

The question of who should be responsible for .se has been a subject of debate in Sweden on several occasions. Before 1997, few had given the issue much thought. When a new organization was needed, people started to discuss alternative ways of handling the governance of the domain. When a nonprofit organization assumed responsibility, some saw the loss of a potential business opportunity, while others believed that .se was a natural issue for the state to deal with. A government-sponsored study of .se published in 2000 expressed the view that the Swedish government should have greater insight into the .se domain, for example, by having representatives on the II Foundation's board of directors.[7]

Although the government has not chosen to become actively involved in .se, the II Foundation maintains regular contact with the various departments and authorities concerned. Meetings also take place under the auspices of ICANN, in which the Swedish government is represented through the Governmental Advisory Council.

As a private nonprofit organization, the II Foundation obtains its revenues from a percentage of the annual fees paid by domain name holders. The II

Foundation formed a company, Network Information Centre Sweden AB (NIC-SE), to handle the day-to-day running of the .se domain.[8] NIC-SE works with more than 200 different registrars who handle contacts with users when new registrations are processed. Until 1997, there was no fee for registering a .se domain name. This is because the work involved was conducted largely on a nonprofit basis and received partial support from the Royal Institute of Technology in Stockholm and the Swedish University Network. In 1998, when II-stiftelsen and NIC-SE were formed, an annual fee of 250 Swedish krona (U.S.$25) was introduced to enable the more organized and professional running of the registry. The fee has remained the same since that time. The goal of the II Foundation is to keep the cost low enough to ensure that no one is prevented from choosing a .se domain and high enough to ensure that .se can be run in a professional manner and keep a high technical quality.

For the first people who registered domain names in Sweden, .se was the natural choice. At that time, only a small number of people were interested in domain names; the Internet was still essentially an idealistic movement. As awareness of and interest in the Internet increased and the Internet and the World Wide Web became commercially attractive, more individuals and companies wanted their own domain names. By this time, because many Swedes were frustrated by the strict regulations that were applied to .se, not all Swedes automatically chose to register domains in the .se name space.

The Swedish ccTLD administrators, like those in France and Belgium, for example, chose to govern .se under a system of prior assessment. This means that to receive a domain name, an applicant had to produce a registered title to the name he or she wanted to register. This process is similar those that, for example, require a birth certificate and utility bill to get a driver's license. In contrast to the prior assessment model, domains like .com, Denmark's .dk, and Italy's .it have few requirements for domain name applications.[9]

The early strict registration policies were an expression of concern that .se should be a domain where users should feel assured that the holder of a .se domain was a serious, existing company. Because specific domain names were limited, the strict rules ensured that a company's name was available when it wanted to register it. But as Internet use grew and domain names became an everyday issue for a large proportion of users, the policy was seen as obsolete; it was abandoned in April 2003, when the new liberalized .se policy was introduced.

The advantage gained from these rules was that a .se website address had acquired a hallmark of seriousness because web users knew that a reputable company was behind the name and that there was no question that the website was Swedish. Private individuals, nonregistered companies with trademarks, and others were able to register .se addresses, but they were required to register under a second-level domain. For example, private persons could register sites under .pp.se; trademarks were found under .tm.se. These second-level .se domains have never been particularly popular, however, because with each added level, the domain name becomes unnecessarily complicated. Instead, many private individuals and others have registered domain names with other TLDs, particularly .com and .nu.

The II Foundation board's official vision and goals for the .se domain notes, "The TLD .se shall be the natural home address for all users who have links to Sweden. This is to be achieved without jeopardizing, or impeding future technical developments or the creation of new services. The domain shall be characterized by stability and reliability, while its administration shall be fast, flexible, predictable and non-bureaucratic."[10]

This vision reflects the desire for a stable operation for the .se domain after the handover from Björn Eriksen, a man who at the end of his tenure had a tough task to manage .se on his own. The vision also implies a wish not to do anything too hastily since there were still uncertainties on how domain names would develop globally.

Thoughtful decision making may be regarded as a typical Swedish cultural characteristic. A similar level of caution was used both when Sweden decided to join the European Union and during the debate on whether Sweden should join the European Monetary Union. Sweden also used to have a restrictive and complex system of laws relating to foreign investment in Sweden, but these rules, like the domain name registration rules, were also recently liberalized.[11]

Until the liberalization of the .se rules, the guiding principle for the .se domain had been that whoever owned the rights to a name should also be able to register the name as a domain name under .se. For example, the Swedish automotive manufacturer Volvo should be able to obtain the domain name volvo.se, while the furniture company IKEA should be able to obtain ikea.se. Users should have confidence that there is a legitimate entity/person behind a .se domain. While this does not eliminate the possibility of fraud and other illegal acts on the Internet, it certainly reduces them.

Geographic names have also been protected so that the organization that best represents a place can be assured of securing the domain name. Each of the Swedish municipalities, for example, has its name registered as a domain name. Thus, Stockholm has stockholm.se, and Göteborg has goteborg.se. During the recent regulatory transition, the Swedish Association of Local Authorities was given a chance to reserve a list of geographic names that it may want to use later. This was done to provide a smoother transition to the new policy.

The rules governing .se have also prohibited misleading, offensive, or confusing domain names. The relatively strict rules governing .se were established to protect companies, municipalities, and other organizations that had not yet become aware of the Internet's potential. While other ccTLDs have adopted similar regulations, each TLD has the opportunity to draft its own rules. The Stockholm Municipality, which had its .se domain reserved, learned this to its detriment when a pornography company registered stockholm.com to market the city from a somewhat different perspective from that generally adopted by the tourist authorities.[12] The municipality has lost numerous attempts to gain control of the domain but continues to demand the domain.

The effect of the strict regulations was efficiency but also less interest in .se. A number of Swedish companies with international operations instead opted for other TLDs. The rise in .com registrations from Swedes was not particularly surprising because .com was the popular domain of the time. Of greater interest is the enormous competition from fellow ccTLD .nu, which is named for the South Pacific island nation of Niue (see chapter 7).

"Nu" means "now" in Swedish; the .nu domain connotes a modern awareness that has appealed to many Swedish individuals. In addition, there is no prior assessment system for .nu; this enables registrants to establish .nu domain names without the difficulties associated with .se.

It is difficult, if not impossible, to find reliable statistics on the size of each TLD's market share in Sweden. Only .se publishes its total number of domain names, though a report suggests that in 1999 the number of Swedish registrations of .nu domains grew from 8,000 to 30,000.[13] In September 2002, .nu said it had 72,000 Swedish domain name holders.[14] The Royal Library in Stockholm has produced a unique database archive of Swedish websites as part of a cultural heritage project. On a number of occasions, project workers have used an automatic search engine of their own design to search for Swedish websites.[15]

While the number of websites does not, of course, indicate how many domain names are in use, it does provide an indication of market shares. Nearly 42,000 Swedish websites were found during the autumn of 1998, two-thirds of which were registered in the .se name space.[16] Three years later, during 2001, nearly 126,000 Swedish websites were found; .se's share had declined from 67 to 45 percent, while .com accounted for 33 percent and .nu for 12 percent.[17] No more recent comparison exists at the time of this writing, but it is likely that the evening-out process has continued.

By the late 1990s, each of the domains had developed its own personality in the eyes of the Swedish public. The .se had come to symbolize Sweden and to be seen as a hallmark of serious intent; this was reflected by the educational and governmental institutions found in the .se name space. The .se domain also had a symbolic association with Sweden. The Swedish Broadcasting Corporation, for example, broadcasts a cultural magazine program called "kulturen.se" (culture.se), the aim of which is to reflect cultural activities throughout Sweden. While for Swedes .se connotes Sweden, .com represents an international image, and .nu, which is used by many private individuals, is connected to organizations and campaigns.

Still, despite its relatively small size and attempt to protect itself from such situations, .se has had problems with domain names that have already been claimed. A typical example occurred in 2000, when Sweden introduced a new pension system called PPM. The natural choice of domain name for the information website would have been ppm.se, but this name had already been registered by the Swedish company Potato Processing Machinery. Instead of appearing under another domain name within the .se name space, information about the pension system can now be found under .nu at the site www.ppm.nu.

When the flow of news items about the pension system was at its peak, the potato machinery company had many bewildered visitors to its website. This example illustrates both the problem of finding unique addresses and how logical it is for Swedes to regard .nu as a natural second choice to .se. When Swedes try to guess web addresses, they usually try out .se, .com, and .nu as the TLD following the likely name.

The .se organization conducted an unpublished attitude survey among the registrars to find out how they and the end customers regard .se relative to other TLDs in Sweden. The survey revealed that the .se domain is viewed as a serious, stable, and well-ordered TLD. It also showed that many people who would like to register under .se could not because of the domain's strict rules.

Perhaps because of its serious character, .se has not been used in company names to the same extent as .com; it has thus avoided being tainted by the reputation of .coms as somewhat naive fortune hunters. The Swedish fashion website and company boo.com is probably one of the best-known Swedish .coms; it suffered the fate of many .coms and went bankrupt in 2000.[18]

In the spring of 2002, more than 100,000 domain names had been registered in the .se name space.[19] The most significant factor for the .se organization was not the actual number of domain names but rather that it be large enough to continue as the natural first choice for users with links to Sweden.

There is no question that the .se domain had excellent stability—among other measures designed to guarantee stable Internet connectivity, the domain had four dedicated Domain Name System servers installed in underground chambers in various locations in Sweden. The technical and administrative operation of .se also functioned smoothly. On the other hand, many questioned the notion that .se was the natural home address for all users with links to Sweden.

Recognizing that this goal had not quite been achieved, the Swedish government initiated several studies to analyze the policies and use of .se. Both reports recommended more liberal rules for .se. These proposals culminated in a series of changes to the .se registration procedures that relax many of the obstacles to registration.

The most recent reorganization—the largest to affect .se since the II Foundation assumed responsibility for the domain—has been the focus of considerable attention. In April 2003, less restrictive registration rules were instituted. Under the new rules, there is no prior assessment; applicants no longer have to prove they are entitled to use a name before they register it. Private people are now able to register directly under .se instead of .pp.se, and there is no limit to the number of domains one can register.[20] In addition, .se also introduced a simplified dispute resolution system to take care of any domain name disputes that arise. The policy is similar to the Uniform Dispute Resolution Policy, operated by ICANN.

While most people welcomed the change, not everyone approved. Some opponents claimed that .se was in danger of being reduced to a TLD just like any other and that it would become more difficult to maintain its image of seriousness and order.[21] Advocates of the change, on the other hand, maintained that .se had the opportunity to become a TLD serving all Swedes, not just Swedish companies.

The .se domain is still dominant in Sweden, and the total number of domain names will continue to increase with the continued liberalization of policies. At the same time, it needs to be borne in mind that Sweden is a small country. Even if everyone in the nation gets his or her own domain name, there is no way .se will be even close to .com, for instance, in size.

On the other hand, liberalization of the rules could increase interest in using .se domains in the Swedish-speaking areas of Finland or among Swedish organizations abroad that wish to emphasize their links with Sweden. In Finland, Swedish is an official language together with Finnish, and there are several hundred thousand Finns whose mother tongue is Swedish. However, this still translates into a relatively small number of potential domains. The more relaxed registration procedures were incorporated to further provide a home for all Swedish websites, be they corporate or personal.

At the time of this writing, the full effect of the new liberalized rules for .se has not yet been seen, but there has been a heightened interest from the public and from companies to register new .se domain names. There is no reason to believe that .se will not remain the top-level domain of choice for

Swedish users. While some argue that the changes in policy could have been made much earlier, one of the reasons for the code's popularity is that it got a reputation of high quality during the times of a more strict policy.

The strict rules served .se well during the development phase but became obsolete as Internet awareness and web maturity grew. Relaxing the registration requirements for .se has given the Swedish people the opportunity to truly populate their home code. Time will tell how successful the move was.

Notes

1. See, for example, "World Competitiveness Report 2002," International Telecommunication Union, presented by the Invest in Sweden Agency, and "Scandinavia Takes the Lead in Fourth Annual Economist Intelligence Unit E-Readiness Rankings," Economist Intelligence Unit, April 1, 2003, http://store.eiu.com/index.asp?layout=pr_story&press_id=890000689&ref=pr_list [accessed May 18, 2003].

2. See, for example, "IDC/World Times Survey, Information Society Index 2002," presented by the Invest in Sweden Agency.

3. "Report 2000:30+11," II Foundation, http://naring.regeringen.se/propositioner_mm/sou/pdf/sou2000_30e.pdf [accessed February 18, 2003].

4. "Growth Statistics for .se" (in Swedish), NIC-SE, www.nic.se/domaner/tillvaxt.shtml [accessed February 18, 2003].

5. See note 4.

6. II-stiftelsen home page at www.iis.se [accessed February 18, 2003].

7. See note 3.

8. NIC-SE home page at www.nic-se.se/english [accessed February 18, 2003].

9. See, for example, AFNIC (French Network Information Center), the registrar for .fr, at www.nic.fr [accessed February 18, 2003]; DNSbe, the registrar for .be, at www.dns.be/eng/index.shtml [accessed February 18, 2003]; DIFO, the registrar for .dk, at www.dk-hostmaster.dk [accessed February 18, 2003]; and the Italian Naming Authority at www.nic.it [accessed February 18, 2003].

10. This was decided by the II Foundation's board in November 1999; see "Protokoll från styrelsemöte nr 15," www.iis.se/iisprot15.shtml [accessed February 18, 2003].

11. United States Department of Commerce, "National Trade Data Bank, Sweden Investment Climate Statement," September 3, 1999, www.tradeport.org/ts/countries/sweden/climate.html [accessed February 18, 2003].

12. "Stockholm Fears Web Porn Label," CNN.com, July 5, 2002, www.cnn.com/2002/TECH/internet/07/05/stockholm.name [accessed February 18, 2003].

13. Lauri Pappinen, "Swedes Abandoning .SE Country Code," InternetNews.com, December 14, 1998, at www.internetnews.com/bus-news/article.php/6_39901 [accessed February 18, 2003].

14. .NU Domain Ltd, "SE-domän VD går till huvudkonkurrenten .NU," press release, www.nu/about/darnell.cfm [accessed February 18, 2003].

15. See Kulturarw3 home page at www.kb.se/kw3/eng [accessed February 18, 2003].

16. Kulturarw3, "Statistics," www.kb.se/kw3/ENG/Statistics.htm [accessed February 18, 2003].

17. See note 16.

18. See "Top Web Retailer Collapses," BBC News, May 18, 2000, http:// news.bbc.co.uk/1/hi/business/752293.stm [accessed February 18, 2003); see also Ernst Malmsten et al., *Boo Hoo: $135 Million, 18 Months . . . A Dot.Com Story from Concept to Catastrophe* (London: Arrow Books, 2002).

19. Presently unpublished press release from NIC-SE.

20. "New .se Rules—Summary," II-stiftelsen, November 2002, www.iis.se/pdf/ New_rules_summary [accessed February 18, 2003].

21. Such comments were made during debates at public hearings arranged by the II Foundation.

~

CHAPTER SEVEN

Niue's .NU: Providing a Free Internet to an Isolated Nation

Richard StClair

The registration of top-level domains is not only a cultural enterprise but also a business. Domain name registration has become competitive; while some codes seek to create a virtual manifestation of their physical borders within their name spaces, other are pluralistic and are marketed to the entire world. Regardless of their composition, each of the codes competes for domain name registrations.

Richard StClair is the technical manager of the Internet User's Society Niue, the group that administers .nu, the country code top-level domain for the island of Niue (pronounced "new-way"). When he arrived on the island in 1994, the telephone in his house had a crank on the side, and his phone number was "two longs and a short." Now, funded by the global marketing of .nu, he has created a Niuean technological infrastructure and provides free Internet access for the island's residents.

With a population of less than 1,500, the island of Niue is one of the smallest countries in the world. The name "Niue" is derived from the loose Niuean language translation for "Behold the coconut." A self-governing state, Niue is located in the South Pacific at 169 degrees west longitude and 19 degrees south latitude. While often quoted as being the largest coral atoll in the world, its landmass of roughly 260 square kilometers (100 square miles), which is about one-and-a-half times the size of Washington, D.C., actually makes it one of the smallest countries. With its nearest neighbors,

Tonga and Samoa, roughly 400 miles away, it is also one of the most isolated countries in the world.[1]

The island's remoteness highlights both the need for global communication and the inherent difficulties in attaining it. Connecting the island of Niue to the global Internet was both technically and economically difficult. However, the marketing of Niue's country code top-level domain (ccTLD), .nu, made it possible to provide the Niuean people with not only free islandwide Internet access but also an Internet café in the capital city of Alofi.

In 1992, on retiring from my position as a Silicon Valley geek-entrepreneur, I had visions of going to the California mountains and fishing for trout. I lasted about a week before I was bored out of my mind. Since childhood, I had always wanted to join the United States Peace Corps; seeking the opportunity to change my perspective on the world, I decided to join the Peace Corps. After the two-year application process, I was on my way to Nigeria. At the time I was due to head out, Nigeria was in the midst of civil war, and fearing a hostage situation, the Peace Corps would not let me go. The next assignment that arose was to go to Niue; I went as a bulldozer mechanic.

The idea was to get away from computers, and, for a short time, that is what I did. About three months into my term on Niue, someone from the government of Niue came down to the workshop where I was putting a transmission in a bulldozer and asked me whether I knew anything about computers because the system at the Treasury Department had crashed. So, of course, I went down and fixed it. This, however, meant that the cat was out of the bag; they now knew that I was a computer guy. I soon transferred from the heavy plant to the Administration Department and began to take care of their computer needs.

I was a member of the first Peace Corps group dispatched to Niue to work with agriculture, business, education, and, of course, information technology in early 1995. This was at a time when news of "this new Internet thing" was spreading throughout the Pacific. The people of Niue, like many others in the world at the time, had many questions about what the Internet, as a communications tool, could do for Niue.

The ability to communicate is important for Niueans because most Niueans do not live on the island of Niue. Many families separate as their members seek employment opportunities abroad. Most of the jobs on the island are for the government; not everyone wants to work for the government or work in the public sector, so they move to other nations, such as New Zealand, Australia, and the United States.

International communication is also a vital way to break through the isolation. The longtime residents of Niue recall that when the airport was built in the 1970s, there was a mass exodus to New Zealand. International phone calls are expensive. It costs NZ$1.90 (U.S.$1.08) a minute to call New Zealand, and NZ$4.20 (U.S.$2.38) a minute to call most other places.[2] Having a free communications system that anyone and everyone had access to would improve personal as well as business and governmental communications.

Unfortunately, the technology on the island was not Internet friendly. There were close to 100 computers in various government departments as well as a few private sector computer owners who used them mainly for word processing, accounting, and the occasional "Duke Nukem" computer game.

Local telephone communication was, however, substandard. In most outer villages, there were small phones with cranks on the sides; my home phone number in Tamakautonga, which was south of Alofi, the capital, was "two longs and a short." In Alofi, there were some Touch-Tone phones, but even these were not capable of any data transmission. The system was too noisy to carry data. While the connections may have sounded clear to a human ear, there was too much noise for the modems to communicate.

In late 1995, Telecom Niue upgraded the phone systems and the switching circuits that handle the local calls; the line noise was reduced, and it was possible to consider electronic communications as a possibility for the island.[3] It did not take long for the locals to recognize the exciting opportunities that lay ahead.

As the technological infrastructure was being built, frequent meetings were held. The government of Niue met with interested parties, which included business owners, computer enthusiasts, and anyone else who wanted to know what "telecommunications" was all about. The meetings showed that Niue was interested in the Internet as a communications tool but had no resources to connect to it or to establish any kind of equipment to build an Internet infrastructure. It was simply too costly for a relatively small number of people to bear the cost of direct links to the outside world for the purpose of Internet services.

In 1997, the government of Niue declared that it had no funds for such a project and decided to delegate its development to the private sector. This decision did not come as a surprise.

The government's priorities at the time were tourism and developing private sector businesses to reduce the large number of public servants—priorities that remain to this day. It was understandable that they did not want to invest in something that had an uncertain future regardless of how exciting it appeared to be. This hesitation was mirrored throughout the world; few on the planet wanted to take the risk.

As my Peace Corps term expired, the Niuean government requested that I stay as a permanent resident to develop the services as best I could with what resources I had at the time. I was given a choice of going back to California to fish for trout or doing something useful that the people of Niue really wanted. The decision to stay was easy. Niue is now my home; like all Niueans, I have the New Zealand citizenship to prove it.

In 1901, New Zealand annexed Niue; for seventy years, Niue was under the protection of the British Empire. Then, in 1974, as part of a larger movement to liberate many of the small island nations, Niue was granted independence in free association with New Zealand. This means that Niue is self-governing, but its residents hold New Zealand citizenship.[4]

As soon as it was possible to carry data on local phone lines after the Telecom Niue upgrades, it was time for the first steps. The ultimate goal was to build a network on Niue for the purpose of carrying Internet services. While there were no resources to connect any such network to the rest of the world, I recognized that sometimes things have to be done one step at a time.

January 1995 marked the debut of Niue's first computer network, which we called the Savage Island Network.[5] This is in homage to the name that British explorer Captain James Cook gave the island when he landed in 1774. As he came ashore, he encountered native people who threw a stone and a spear. Interpreting the actions negatively, he named Niue "Savage Island." The name, however, is a misnomer. The native people saw Cook's arrival as trespass, so they challenged Cook in a welcoming ritual by throwing a spear less than five paces to see if he could catch it and to test whether he was coming in peace.[6]

The Savage Island Network ran twenty-four hours a day, seven days a week, and provided the first electronic communications of its kind on Niue. Because phone lines were rather scarce at the time, we managed to snag three lines for dial-ups to the system. The original system ran as a privately owned standard bulletin board system (BBS) and was configured as a local-only (intranet) e-mail, file server, and BBS service.

Niue's government agency responsible for the internal administrative infrastructure was the primary user of that system. There were also a handful of private sector users interested in data communications. The only problem with the system, which was a nationwide intranet, was that it was not connected to the rest of the world.

With only twenty to thirty users, the privately owned Savage Island Network was the beginning of telecommunications development on Niue. It was a training tool, test bed, and learning environment for the local users as well as those who assumed the challenge of things to come. While the need to be familiar with new technologies was part of its driving force, it was driven mostly by dreams of being connected to the real Internet.

After about a year, that network's workings were replaced with a thirty-two-bit version of the WildCat BBS (BBSs were the computer modem dial-up systems that were used before the Internet was popular). Since there was no Internet connection to the outside world at the time, it was the only system to choose. Fortunately, as a developer and user of BBS systems in the United States, I already had experience running and building them.

With this system, the users found themselves thrust into the graphical world of HTML (Hypertext Markup Language), the language of the World Wide Web, and other vivid interfaces. This allowed us to be one step closer toward achieving the look and feel of the real Internet. Still, it was a local-only BBS running file services, newsgroup bulletin boards, and e-mail.

The BBS created an excellent training ground. People on Niue learned the concepts of using a modem and communicating over a telephone line with something other than their voices. It also familiarized them with browsers and sending and receiving messages. It was a superb practice tool for the larger Internet that was coming. The connection also allowed government departments to exchange data electronically without printing it or traveling to other departments on the island in a motor vehicle.

Running the systems from the living room of my house, I experienced plenty of failures from power surges, lightning, and creepy-crawly things, like geckos and kangaroo rats, that made their way inside the machines. If a gecko, for example, crawls into a live power supply, it will explode when it gets to the high-voltage heat sinks and will usually blow up the power supply in the process. Still, despite occasional failures, the value of the network was beginning to show; both network traffic and the user base constantly increased.

By 1997, the Savage Island Network had reached its limits on what could be developed without resources to connect it to the rest of the world. The days of the self-funded hobby were rapidly coming to an end, and there were no ideas or resources that could be found to make that transition from a nationwide intranet to a full-time connection to the outside world.

Fortunately for Niue, there was a technology developer in the United States who was at the same time taking notice of Niue. J. William Semich was a longtime technology and Internet developer and hobbyist who wanted to work with Niue to build its online infrastructure.

Bill and I share a hobby; we are both ham radio operators. We are both guys who would go out in the rain and set up radios just to see if we could get them to work. In Boston, Bill was developing a plan to form a nonprofit corporation called the Internet Users Society Niue, which would develop and market Niue's ccTLD, .nu, and use much of the profit to build the communications infrastructure on the island of Niue.[7]

Encouraged by the proposal, Niuean government representatives soon introduced Bill to the Savage Island Network. After organizational discussions, the parties agreed that the project would continue as a private sector development. The Savage Island Network would join forces with Bill to form the Internet Users Society Niue to complete the task of bringing worldwide e-mail and Internet services to Niue.

The primary fund-raising would be the development and international marketing of Niue's ccTLD, .nu. Until this plan was developed, no one was interested in the code. In 1995, I had a meeting with the director of Telecom Niue; I told him that the domain was available and that they could write a letter to the Internet Assigned Numbers Authority to have it delegated to them in case they ever wanted to do something with it. He said they knew about the codes. No one requested the delegation of .nu, so it sat for years until we applied for it.

The resources generated by .nu domain name registrations would be used to develop and maintain the Internet services for the people of Niue. It would, it was hoped, bear some of the ongoing costs to make the services cheap enough for Niueans to afford.

The ccTLDs were created with the sole purpose of someday being used to help the host countries, regardless of their ccTLDs, develop their Internet services. As I see it, to date, a number of them have been used to line someone's pocket; Niue is one of the few places on Earth that really does use the domain for what it was intended.

After a lot of hard work and a few minor setbacks in getting the equipment shipped to Niue, we brought the e-mail-only services online. In March 1997, after some weeks of testing, we opened to the Niuean public.

With a growing user base, the e-mail-only trial period demonstrated that there was a real need for communications and that the development of those communications would be a valuable asset to the country of Niue as a whole. The speed and growth of the network was limited only by the lack of available financial resources. Seeing the potential during the initial test-and-observation period, the Internet User's Society set up a full-blown global marketing plan for .nu. It also developed its own infrastructure in the United States and Sweden to continue developing the .nu domain.[8] The time people spent online grew on a steady curve over the first few months and has stayed constant for the past four years. People used to be online for ten to twenty hours per week; now they are online 4,500 hours a week. Each week, we send and receive about 20,000 e-mails in and out of Niue.

To entice possible registrants, we kept names short by allowing registrants to register their domains in the flat .nu name space as opposed to under second-level domains, such as .com.nu or .org.nu. We also kept the registration process simple by allowing registrants to sign up for domain names on our website with little required paperwork and by charging only

U.S.$25 a name, which was cheaper than many ccTLDs as well as .com. It now costs about U.S.$60 for a two-year .nu registration. We have chosen to use the Uniform Dispute Resolution Policy to resolve domain name registration complaints.[9]

Sweden is the largest market for .nu domain names. We targeted domain name registrants from Sweden because "nu" means "now" in Swedish; we believe it had a certain appeal to the market for that reason. While "nu" also means "naked" in French, to this day we have very few domains registered by French nationals.

By January 1999, there were enough financial resources generated by the global registrations of the .nu domains to establish a full-time Frame relay connection from Niue to New Zealand. Frame relay is the full-time satellite digital connection to the backbone of the Niue and New Zealand connection. It is, literally, the connection; it is also the expensive part that I could not afford when I was trying to make the connection on my own. In addition to varying traffic costs, we pay NZ$10,000 (U.S.$5,673) a month for that 64K connection to New Zealand; within New Zealand, a much faster 256K connection costs only NZ$19.00 (U.S.$10.78) a month.

We also built a dedicated building on Niue for the Internet Service Provider (ISP) equipment to be housed and maintained; to prevent the geckos from getting into the system, we built a sealed room next to the satellite downlink location to house the servers. Not only were there enough resources to install the systems and put them online, but also, as it turned out, there were enough to cover the cost of the ongoing maintenance and operational costs. This meant that instead of merely providing cheaper services for residents, the Internet Users Society Niue was able to cover the cost completely, thereby making Internet services free to all Niuean residents. It was an astounding turning point. Because the costs involved in building the connection were so astronomical, we were all surprised that the registrations alone could support it.

We also used the funds to build a public access point (an Internet café) in the Alofi area (where most Niueans live or work) to provide free access. The public access point was designed and built to target Niueans who might not have computers of their own. As a result, the entire population of Niue has access to the Internet.

Open from 9 A.M. to 3 P.M., Monday through Friday, the public access point is constantly used. While the locals are the primary users, many yachtsmen can be found using the services during the yachting season; at season's peak, there will be as many as thirty anchored yachts in the water. While there is no specific event to come for, many yachts stop on Niue for a couple of weeks while out exploring the world. Yachting season is any time of the year when it is not cyclone season, usually from April to September; because there are no lagoons on Niue, there are few places to hide from a cyclone.

While there are not a great number of tourists to Niue, flights do arrive from Samoa and New Zealand twice a week. Tourists and consultants to the island who are enjoying their stays or waiting for a flight out also find their way into the offices to check their e-mail.

Because .nu domain name registrations fund these services, the people of Niue do not have to pay for Internet access. The significance of this should not be underestimated; if access were not free, the cost of equipment maintenance and of connecting to the Internet from such an isolated location would be prohibitive.

Considering the connection costs, it is remarkable that the marketing of the ccTLD can pay the cost of developing and maintaining Internet services for an entire nation. Niue's size and population, along with its people's willingness to grasp new ideas and desire to be online, have contributed to the success of the .nu project.

Now after several years with full Internet services, Niueans see the Internet as a standard communications utility. Internet use is as common as the telephone, hot and cold running water, and electricity. In fact, there are probably a few Niueans who have e-mail addresses but do not have hot and cold running water.

The free Internet services have reunited many people who have been isolated from their families who are living overseas. Some expatriate Niueans have met members of their "on Niue" families for the first time, while others have made trips to Niue to finally meet family and see Niue for the first time. This is one example of the Internet truly achieving what many hoped it would: the elimination of the tyranny of distance.

In the public sector, the Internet has been a valuable tool to enable instantaneous communication with overseas aid organizations. It has substantially helped to coordinate many regional development projects. Going beyond the scope of the raw communications, we have set up an advisory council of Niuean residents who can vote on proposals that are submitted online by virtually anyone on Niue. In meetings, the council reviews the proposals and decides how best to serve the Niuean community with whatever resources are available.

Niue has had full Internet services since June 1999. The systems continue to improve. There have been fewer than eight hours of downtime in four years; those hours were the result of the local power company shutting down the power to replace transformers, during which time, for safety concerns, we also had to shut down. As a result, the system rivals any ISP on Earth.

The services have been opened to all permanent Niuean residents and the government of Niue at no cost. Internet traffic has increased, and the hardware is state of the art. With continued worldwide support of .nu, the information technology development on Niue can continue as planned.

To this day, this is the only ccTLD model of its kind—a model that generates and contributes enough resources to keep an entire country online with free services. With more than 100,000 domain name registrations, persistent hard work and a little luck will enable .nu to continue to produce the funds to keep Niue online and connected to the world for many years to come.

Notes

1. For more statistical information about Niue, see Central Intelligence Agency, "Niue," *The World Factbook*, www.cia.gov/cia/publications/factbook/geos/ne.html [accessed March 4, 2003].

2. Niue does not have its own currency; it uses New Zealand dollars.

3. For more information about telecommunications in Niue, see, for example, "National Policy on Telecommunications for Niue," First Draft, November 2002, www.gov.nu/telecom/policy.htm#_Toc25664221 [accessed March 4, 2003].

4. See, for example, Internet Users Society Niue at www.niue.nu [accessed March 12, 2003], Niue Island at www.niueisland.nu [accessed March 12, 2003], and Weekly Niue News at www.niuenews.nu [accessed March 12, 2003].

5. See "History," Internet Users Society Niue, www.niue.nu/iusn/history.htm [accessed March 12, 2003].

6. "Niue History Past & Present Commemorating 100 Years Niue-New Zealand Association," NiueIsland.com, www.niueisland.com/100/history.htm [accessed March 12, 2003].

7. Internet Users Society Niue at www.niue.nu/iusn [accessed March 12, 2003].

8. See the NuNames home page at www.nunames.nu [accessed March 12, 2003].

9. See "Uniform Dispute Resolution Policy," NuNames, www.nunames.nu/udrp.htm [accessed March 4, 2003].

~

CHAPTER EIGHT

Moldova's .MD:
The Little Domain That Roared

Dana M. Gallup

Enabling the construction of a technological infrastructure on the island of Niue, the licensing of .nu is one of many stories about commercially marketed domain names. While .nu has appealed to Swedish speakers, another code, Moldova's .md, has appealed to English speakers. While the combination of letters has no meaning in Moldova's official language, Moldovan (which is similar to Romanian and Russian), in the United States .md was expected to have a definite appeal to doctors looking for an ideal presence on the Internet.

Having drafted the original agreement between the Moldovan administrator and his American company, Florida-based attorney Dana M. Gallup was one of the earliest entrants into the domain name game. The Moldovan administrator granted him and his business partner the rights to license .md domains with the hopes of raising revenue and lifting the nation of Moldova from its struggling economy. His experiences reflect not only the economic and technological struggles posed by the marketing of domain names but also the intensely political power struggles that occur as a result.

"Come meet me for lunch tomorrow."

That is how my adventure into the domain name business began. The lunch proposal came from a client of mine, John Harris, whom I had begun representing about a year or so earlier while he was in the housing construction business. By the time John sought my legal assistance in late 1995, his business was failing. He had paid me for most of the work I had done to defend his interests, but he had still owed me about $10,000 in legal fees after all the claims had been resolved.

I understood that the construction business had severely beaten John down financially and emotionally, so I never pressed him too hard for the money he owed me. I would send him invoices, and he would repeatedly assure me that he would pay me when he could. I continued to send him bills after I relocated my practice from southwestern Florida to Miami in 1997, and he continued to provide assurances that I would someday be paid.

When John called and asked me to join him for lunch, my first inclination was to politely decline. After all, the drive from Miami to his home in Bonita Springs is about two hours each way. That is a long way to go for lunch. As I started my polite declination, however, John added more intrigue to the invitation. "I have something very exciting to discuss with you," he said. "A proposal. It's a very big idea. This will be worth your time."

He had aroused my entrepreneurial curiosity. I agreed to meet him for lunch.

When John answered his front door, I saw a look of excitement and energy that had been notably absent from his face since I had known him. Over lunch, he began to unravel his "big idea."

He explained that he had recently traveled to Canada to attend his father's funeral; the tremendous grief he felt had left him in a particularly contemplative mood as he traveled back to Florida. During the return plane ride, John noticed that in Canadian advertisements the companies were not just using domain names ending in .com. Instead, many Internet companies in Canada were using .ca., the country code top-level domain (ccTLD) designation for Canada.

As he sat on the long plane ride home from Canada, still awash in grief and looking for a distraction, John's thoughts returned to .ca. Suddenly, it hit him.

"CA—postal code for California!"

He thought that businesses and individuals in California would love to have websites that identified them as Californians. Not knowing anything about domain names, he wondered whether there was a way to market .ca in California.

His mind flooded with questions. Who owned or controlled .ca? Who could he contact to make a business proposal of this? More to the point, what exactly was .ca anyway? How was it different from .com? His mind began reeling. It proved to be a welcome distraction from the grief.

As we ate our lunch, John went on with his story. He had trouble sleeping the night after he returned from Canada because he kept thinking about .ca for California; he kept wondering about the potential commercial value of such an undertaking, though he doubted that Canada would have any real interest in sharing its domain with California.

During that night and the days that followed, John researched domain names and learned the answers to many of the questions he had posed on that flight. John then learned about the differences between the three-letter generic top-level domains (gTLDs) and two-lettered ccTLDs. Canada's .ca was a ccTLD that, at the time, was run by the computer science department at Simon Fraser University.[1] It was governed differently from .com but as another Internet address ending served the same function. To commercialize the domain, he would have to assess the interest of the specific code's administrator. He learned about the U.S. Department of Commerce's role as the controlling government authority that delegated at least some policymaking and technical control over the Domain Name System to the Internet Assigned Numbers Authority (IANA). He became familiar with RFC 1591, a document that laid out the guidelines for ccTLDs, and about the hundreds of other ccTLDs that were assigned to countries and regions around the world.[2]

At this point in our lunch, John pulled out a list to show me. Printed from IANA's website, the list contained each of the ccTLD extensions, along with the country or region assigned to the domain and the information for the administrative and technical contacts. "I have identified twenty-eight ccTLDs with abbreviations that match postal codes for states in the United States," John explained. He pointed out Gabon's .ga for Georgia, the Cayman Islands' .ky for Kentucky, and Moldova's .md for Maryland.

".MD for Maryland," I interrupted. "Forget Maryland. Do you realize what .md also means?" I waited until I saw the answer come across his face.

"Doctors!" we exclaimed in unison.

As we looked at the list again, we began to see other commercial uses for the ccTLDs. For example, Micronesia's .fm and Armenia's .am for radio stations, Tuvalu's .tv for the television networks, and Panama's .pa for lawyers and accountants. Now I was getting excited. I asked, "Do you think anyone else has figured this out?"

John replied, "Don't know, but I do know we should act on this quickly because it is only a matter of time until others do figure it out." John was right to act quickly. In 1999, just eight months after beginning his contact with administrators, in exchange for a 20 percent stake and $50 million over twelve years, the government of the South Pacific island nation of Tuvalu granted the Los Angeles–based .tv Corporation the exclusive right to register .tv domains for ten years.[3]

John's proposal to me was quite straightforward. We would work together as partners in an effort to acquire marketing rights for commercially viable ccTLDs like .md. My role would be to draft contracts, to research any legal issues involved in the endeavor, and to assist in the search for venture capital by setting up some meetings with associates of mine who might be interested in investing. John offered me an equal equity interest to his and requested that, in exchange for such a substantial equity interest, I agree to forgive the balance owed in attorney's fees for the work. Because I was quite excited by the possibilities, I readily agreed to the deal.

John went to work on reaching out to the various ccTLD administrators, while I began to reach out to investors and organize the corporate structure of the business. We chose to call the business Domain Name Trust, Inc., or DNT for short. The name was intended to reflect both the possibility of acquiring rights to more than one domain and the belief that domains and the Internet as a whole did not necessarily belong to any one entity but were instead held in "trust" for the use and benefit of the community as a whole.

Within two months, John received a positive response from the administrator of .md, a gentleman named Pavel Chirev. Chirev was the administrative contact for the .md domain since the ccTLD was delegated to the Republican Centre for Informatics (RCI; now called MoldData State Enterprise) in October 1994. He managed RCI and agreed to meet with John in his homeland; I quickly drafted an agreement for John to take with him.

Located between Romania and Ukraine, the former Soviet republic of Moldova is one of Europe's poorest nations. The 4.5 million people who live in the country earn an average monthly salary of just U.S.$30. According to Amnesty International, close to 80 percent of the population lives below the poverty line.[4] In 1999, there were two Internet Service Providers (ISPs) in Moldova.[5] These realities, along with an outdated telephone system, made the offer to market Moldova's ccTLD all the more attractive.

In drafting the agreement, I began to grapple with some of the legal concepts inherent in the ccTLD structure. Given the information available on IANA's website, including the text of RFC 1591, it was apparent that a ccTLD administrator did not necessarily hold any "ownership" rights in the ccTLD.[6] Yet, the administrator did have fairly wide authority and discretion to set policies and procedures for the domain and to determine issues such as making registration of the domain open or closed to those outside the nation's borders, choosing to make the domain commercial or noncommercial, and determining the level of access to the domain. It seemed to me, therefore, that the administrator occupied the legal status of a licensee, while IANA (or arguably the Department of Commerce) could be viewed as the licensor. In other words, notwithstanding the rhetoric in RFC 1591 suggesting that no one owned the Internet and domain names, it seemed to me that domain names (and the Internet as well) were "owned" and "controlled" by the U.S. government through the Department of Commerce and

IANA. In turn, IANA delegated certain rights and responsibilities over a domain to the appointed administrator, much in the same way as the Federal Communications Commission grants a license to a radio station to operate at a certain defined frequency. Like a radio station owner, a domain administrator was then empowered to enter agreements with third parties to exploit the rights that had been granted.

Given this construct, I prepared an agreement that was most closely akin to a license (or sublicense) agreement. The agreement called for our company, DNT, to hold the exclusive right to market and register domain names under .md in most areas of the world for twenty-five years. Moldova's RCI would receive just under 10 percent of the revenue received by DNT for each domain name registered.[7] The agreement also called for designation of a DNT representative as the technical administrative contact and relocation of the primary Domain Name Server (DNS) to the United States. In this way, DNT could maintain technical operational control of the domain and ensure the quality and speed of the Internet connection during the domain name registration process. The agreement was purposely kept short and simple in form, in part so that we could avoid confusing Chirev with American legal jargon and in part to keep the relationship flexible so that adjustments could be made in the future given the relatively new ground on which we were treading.

After John's two trips to Moldova and a substantial amount of negotiation with Chirev, we were able to secure an agreement with RCI in May 1998. Interestingly, another person from the United States had contacted Chirev at about the same time as John made contact. Chirev, intending to respond to John, inadvertently sent this other person an invitation to meet with him in Moldova. That person arrived in Moldova a few days before John and offered Chirev U.S.$1 for every name registered. By contrast, John proposed that RCI be paid U.S.$15 for each name registered, which at the time was approximately double the wholesale value of a .com name. About sixty days after John first went to Moldova, another interested party approached Chirev with a proposal regarding .md, thus reaffirming our presumption that we were not the only people in the world who had figured out the commercial application for .md.

With the agreement in place, we were able to convince a handful of friends and family—those who I would later learn are referred to as the "angel" investors by venture capitalists—to invest in our business. We were able to raise a total of $120,000, and for that investment, John and I surrendered 50 percent of the company to the investors.

In the weeks that followed, John prepared for the transfer by buying the necessary equipment and requesting the technical changes from IANA, the domain name governing body. John purchased the hardware and software needed to run the DNS, a distributed database system that translates textual host names to numerical IP (Internet Protocol) addresses. We then sought and received authorization from IANA to designate a DNT representative as the technical administrator of .md and to redelegate, or repoint, the DNS to our facility in the United States. After this was accomplished, we were ready to open our cyberdoors for business.

We set the price for a one-year registration of a .md domain name at U.S.$299. This was considerably higher than the cost of generic domain names under .com or .net, which were each U.S.$35 per year. However, our rationale was that .md was a niche domain with an elite target market of health care providers. In addition, as part of the registration, we included web hosting and e-mail addresses associated with the registered domain name.

Much to our surprise and delight, within days of opening the .md registration service to the public, we began receiving registration orders. The interesting thing, however, was that the first registrations did not come from our target market of health care providers. Rather, the first registrations came from Internet entrepreneurs, followed by cybersquatters and Fortune 1000 companies. As we would quickly learn, a tremendous market existed for the registration of trademarks by companies seeking to avoid having their names registered by name speculators and those who became known as cybersquatters. A speculator was someone who registered a generic non-proprietary name, such as insurance.md, with the hopes that someone would see tremendous value in the name and pay the registrant substantial fees to acquire it. A cybersquatter, by contrast, was someone who registered a proprietary name, such as mayoclinic.md, with the expectation that the legal holder of the proprietary name would pay the registrant for the domain name instead of litigating the issue of whether the registration violated the proprietary rights of the trademark holder. We quickly discovered that, indeed, the largest category of registrants was the speculators and cybersquatters.

In the months that followed, we registered thousands of domains, mostly to companies seeking to protect their trademarks and to the speculators hoping to register a name with perceived value. As the registration numbers grew, we realized that our business model was proving to be a success. We then turned our attention from the maintenance of the domain to its governance.

As we became more involved in the world of domain names, we learned that a new organization had been formed—the Internet Corporation for Assigned Names and Numbers (ICANN)—which was assuming the regulatory roles of IANA. In an effort to organize its structure and ultimately to assume the functions of IANA and define policies and procedures relating to all aspects of top-level domains, ICANN was holding meetings at various locations around the world. Because we perceived that additional restrictions and regulations on ccTLDs could have a negative impact on our business, we felt it was important to closely monitor ICANN's activity and to attend its conferences.

The first ICANN conference John and I were able to attend was in Berlin in May 1999. In reviewing the agenda and schedule for the meeting, I noted that one of the critical constituencies formed by ICANN was the Governmental Advisory Committee (GAC). While most of the other constituencies appeared to be loose hodgepodges of various interested groups, GAC was by far the most clearly defined and organized. Participation in GAC meetings was restricted to designated representatives of a sovereign government and one observer selected by the government representative. Interestingly, however, some nongovernmental entities, such as the World Intellectual Property Organization, were allowed to attend GAC meetings.[8]

Prior to attending the Berlin conference, we asked RCI whether Moldova would be sending a representative to the GAC meeting. RCI responded that Moldova did not have enough funds to send a representative but would grant me the authorization to attend the conference on behalf of Moldova. Armed with a letter of authorization from the government of Moldova, John and I went to Berlin, and I sat at the table with representatives from approximately twenty-three other countries at the GAC meeting. Unlike every other constituency meeting, the GAC meeting was completely closed to the public. I found this to be rather ironic. Given the fact that ICANN was an outgrowth of the Department of Commerce, it seemed to me that its meetings should be conducted in an open forum to be viewed by the public at large.

During the morning session of the GAC meeting, I listened as the then chairperson, Dr. Paul Twomey of Australia, laid out the agenda for discussion.[9] Twomey has since been appointed ICANN's president and chief executive officer.[10] The morning agenda included, among other things, the recommendation of policies to the ICANN board of directors for the restriction of commercial use of ccTLDs. Such restrictions were strongly supported by the representatives of the larger countries, such as England, France, and the United States. Unfortunately, many of the smaller countries, including those like Moldova who had allowed commercial use of their ccTLDs, were not present at the GAC meeting, though the reason for their absence was unclear.

As the morning session continued, I felt that it was important to articulate the position of those countries such as Moldova that had allowed commercial use of their ccTLDs and who might ultimately derive badly needed revenue from commercial registrations. While I had the attention of the

GAC participants, I also felt it was important to express objection to the closed-door nature of the meeting. Needless to say, neither of the viewpoints I expressed during the morning session was warmly greeted by the representatives for the larger countries. I did, however, receive some general support and appreciation from some representatives from smaller countries.

During the first break of the morning session, Twomey approached me. He indicated that a number of the representatives had expressed concern and objection to my attendance at the GAC meeting. Twomey informed me that I had a conflict of interest because I was at the meeting representing both a government and a commercial entity. I pointed out to Twomey that there were other participants at the meeting who were not government officials and who held positions with commercial enterprises, such as ISPs.

I believe that my dissenting views created an obstruction to GAC's ability to articulate a "consensus" policy to be presented to the ICANN board. Twomey asked whether I would voluntarily remove myself from the meeting. If I did not do so, I would be asked to leave. I rejected Twomey's suggestion, advising him that I was authorized to attend the meeting by the government of Moldova and that is was wrong to banish me from a meeting simply because certain representatives did not share my point of view, just as it was wrong to close the meeting to the public so that the world could not hear GAC's point of view.

Prior to reconvening the meeting, Twomey informed me that a vote was going to be taken to amend the rules for participation in GAC so as to exclude nongovernmental officials with a conflicting commercial interest. I took that to mean that the rules were being amended to kick me out of the meeting. At this point, I was faced with a dilemma. Do I stand my ground and face involuntary removal, perhaps by German authorities, or do I leave peacefully? Fearing the possibility of seeing the inside of a German jail, I chose the latter option and requested that, in exchange for my voluntary removal from the meeting, I be granted permission to summarize my views and concerns on behalf of those ccTLDs like Moldova's that had chosen to open their domains to commercial registration. Twomey granted my request, so I expressed my opinions and left the meeting.[11]

When I walked into the General Assembly room, where all the other completely unorganized constituencies were gathered, I discovered that I had obtained a type of celebrity status. Word had quickly spread about my GAC experience. One person after another approached me and asked whether I was the guy who was kicked out of the GAC meeting. So many of the participants in the General Assembly were curious to know about what was going on behind the closed-door GAC meeting that I eventually stood up before the Assembly and told them what had transpired.

For the rest of the Berlin conference and in conferences that followed in Santiago, Chile, and Los Angeles, I became an advocate for the rights of the ccTLD administrators.[12] This is not to say that I was opposed to governments regulating ccTLDs. I recognize that governments should play a role in the policymaking for a ccTLD. I did, however, object to the notion that a handful of governments or ICANN itself should impose restrictive policies on ccTLD administrators.

As the months went by it became apparent that ICANN, like any new and large bureaucratic entity, was not going to make any definitive policy changes regarding ccTLDs anytime soon. Indeed, ICANN soon had greater concerns, including litigation with domain name registrar Network Solutions, Inc., over control of the registry of generic domains such as .com.[13] ICANN was also consumed by the paramount desire to create new gTLDs and gTLD registrars as well as by questions regarding whether ICANN was the appropriate body to regulate domain names and, if so, the scope of that authority.

With ICANN and its polices seeming to be in a perpetual state of limbo, our company turned its attention to marketing and branding .md and registering as many names as possible. We also turned our attention to raising capital—exploring options ranging from private placement to initial public offerings (IPOs). This, of course, was during the heyday of the .com boom, and because we were an Internet company that was actually showing profit, we were warmly greeted by venture capital groups and brokers alike. Eventually, we decided to work with a broker on a private-placement offering whereby we would hope to raise U.S.$4 million to $8 million to be applied to the growth of our company. According to the broker, after our company developed an appropriate corporate infrastructure and began registering thousands of domain names through our marketing efforts, we could then move forward with an IPO.

As we developed the private-placement memorandum, however, the risk factors associated with our business began to scare the underwriters and even some of our own angel investors. These risk factors included the uncertain legal foundation of our relationship with RCI. We did not officially know whether RCI "owned" the rights to .md and whether it had the right to transfer the rights to our company. We did not know whether ICANN would eventually restrict or prohibit the commercial use of ccTLDs, and we did not know whether the creation of new gTLDs would create too much competition for registrations and lessen the desirability of a niche domain such as .md.

In the end, these risk factors, coupled with the fact that our company did not, in the eyes of the underwriters, appear to have an experienced management team in place to answer the difficult questions, overwhelmed the underwriters. As a result, the private offering never occurred.

Fortunately, just as the private offering was falling apart, we began to receive interest from various suitors looking to acquire the rights we held in .md. Ultimately, the best offer came from a privately held company from Atlanta called MedAscend, Inc., which offered to pay $10 million for our company. Given the risks and uncertainties that were surrounding the world of domain names, the offer seemed simply too good to refuse. On February 14, 2000, MedAscend acquired DNT and assumed the right to market and register .md domain names. At the time of the transfer, approximately 13,000 .md domain names had been registered.[14]

Regrettably, the rest of the ".md story" does not have a happy ending. In purchasing DNT, MedAscend was able to raise millions of dollars in investment capital and several millions more in private loans. However, MedAscend was not able to make a success of .md and was ultimately forced to declare bankruptcy after having depleted its funds.

The failure of MedAscend is likely attributable to many causes. The bursting of the .com bubble beginning in March 2000 (only one month after the sale of DNT) surely had an effect, as did the bear market that set in over the next two years. This effectively dried up sources of capital and closed off lucrative exit strategies, such as an acquisition by a large domain name player like Network Solutions, Inc., or Register.com, Inc.

In addition to the financial problems, MedAscend also faced increasing hostility from the Moldovan government. It viewed the transfer as the theft or hijacking of the country's proprietary rights in .md by a foreign company. The rumblings from the Moldovan government had existed to some extent while we were running DNT, but with each change in leadership in Moldova (of which there were many over the short time we operated DNT), the opposition would ebb and flow. When word spread that DNT had been sold to MedAscend for $10 million, the dissenting voices became louder. Further fuel was added to the fire in Moldova when MedAscend decided that DNT's rather simple contract with RCI was insufficient; MedAscend then attempted to renegotiate its arrangement with RCI and, to that end, tried to secure a new agreement that was complex and contained extensive legalese.

Soon, different factions within and outside Moldova began to fight about who held the rights to .md and at what price, if any, those rights should be transferred. MedAscend, equipped with an arsenal of lawyers and consultants in both the United States and Moldova, tried in vain to secure a new agreement. Interestingly, many of the contract negotiations circumvented .md's administrator Chirev since MedAscend believed it needed to reach agreement directly with the Moldovan government. None too pleased with the actions of MedAscend and believing that RCI was not being paid its share for names registered by MedAscend, Chirev claimed that the company was breaching the original agreement. Though administrative control ultimately remained with Chirev at all times, the Moldovan parliament also got involved by passing legislation regulating the domain.

Shortly after acquiring .md, MedAscend changed its name to Dot MD, Inc., with the wholly owned subsidiary Dot MD, LLC, holding the rights to the DNT agreement. Faced with a mounting firestorm of controversy in Moldova, the inability to secure a new agreement, claims of breaching the old agreement by RCI, and the inability to raise additional capital or otherwise grow the company because of the instability of the financial markets and the instability of the situation in Moldova, MedAscend (Dot MD) filed for bankruptcy protection. Although the principal officers and directors of Dot MD initially hoped to complete a reorganization by filing for bankruptcy under Chapter 11, they soon thereafter walked away from the company. They left the assets of the company, which included the .md agreement, in the hands of a bankruptcy trustee.

In the hands of the trustee, Dot MD has continued to minimally function.[15] However, disputes continue to exist among the various creditor factions and RCI (which has now changed its name to MoldData), which continues to argue that the original agreement was breached. It argues that, as a consequence, the agreement is terminated and of no force and effect. In 2002, there were attempts to liquidate the assets of Dot MD, which included the sale of the .md agreement, but those efforts have been repeatedly thwarted by Moldova's insistence that no rights to sell exist.

To end the perpetual state of uncertainty, in December 2002 the trustee reached a settlement agreement with MoldData. The agreement called for MoldData to pay U.S.$175,000 to the bankruptcy estate, and, in exchange, the estate returned any and all rights under the .md agreement to MoldData.

And so we have come full circle, with the "rights" to .md residing with MoldData under the management of Chirev in Moldova. What began as a seemingly great idea—fueled by a mere U.S.$120,000 in investment capital and peaking with the registration of thousands of domain names and the sale of the company for millions of dollars—appears to have now collapsed into a fire sale of the .md rights back to Moldova for $175,000. Given the risks and uncertainties now surrounding .md, it will be very difficult to regain the prominence this domain once had. It is instead far more likely that the story of .md will end like so many of the great ideas and lofty goals of the .com boom.

As for the domain name game as a whole, from my vantage point it appears that none of the ccTLDs will be able to permeate the market currently monopolized by the generic domains and, particularly, .com. For all the speculation that we would exhaust the .com names, it does not appear that this has happened or is likely to happen anytime soon. While some ccTLDs, such as the Australian territory Cocos (Keeling) Islands' .cc, have been able to register large volumes of names, most companies still establish their primary web presence under .com.[16] I suspect that this will not change for many years to come. John, on the other hand, has remained confident that ccTLD names hold commercial value, and he has since moved forward with the acquisition of rights to other domains, including .sr from the country of Suriname, which he markets to "seniors" around the world.

While I have now removed myself from the domain name business and have returned to the more mundane practice of law, I still look with passing interest on the clashes among the various interest groups within and outside of ICANN, the evolution and standardization of domain name policies, and the successes and failures of other ccTLDs. I do not regret for a moment accepting John Harris's lunch invitation in 1998 and going on the .md adventure that followed. The experience changed and enriched my life in many ways and afforded me a unique insight into the world of domain names.

Notes

1. For more about Canada's .ca, see, for example, Canadian Internet Registration Authority at www.ca [accessed January 19, 2003], and Joyita Haldar and Brian Washburn, "Digital Autonomy—How Canada's Domain Name Became an Exercise in Net Administration," *Teledotcom.com*, June 4, 2001, www.teledotcom.com/article/TEL20010531S0029 [accessed January 19, 2003].

2. The most recent version of the IANA list of ccTLDs is available at www.iana.org/cctld/cctld-whois.htm [accessed January 19, 2003]; see also Jon Postel, "Domain Name System Structure and Delegation" (Network Working Group, Request for Comments No. 1591), March 1994, at www.rfc-editor.org/rfc/rfc1591.txt [accessed January 19, 2003].

3. For more about Tuvalu's .tv, see, for example, The .tv Corporation at www.tv [accessed January 19, 2003], and Polly Sprenger, "In Whose Best Interests?" *The Industry Standard*, May 8, 2000, www.thestandard.com/article/0,1902,14538,00.html [accessed January 19, 2003].

4. "Amnesty International Report 2002: Moldova," Amnesty International, http://web.amnesty.org/web/ar2002.nsf/eur/moldova!Open [accessed January 19, 2003].

5. Central Intelligence Agency, "Moldova," *The World Factbook*, January 1, 2002, www.cia.gov/cia/publications/factbook/geos/md.html [accessed January 19, 2003].

6. See IANA at www.iana.org [accessed January 19, 2003], and Request for Comments No. 1591 at www.rfc-editor.org/rfc/rfc1591.txt [accessed January 19, 2003].

7. See Quest Economics Database, "World of Information Country Report," April 10, 2002, 28, noting, "By early 2000, some 8,000 American doctors had bought the right to use the "md" suffix, raising US$200,000 for Moldova."

8. The complete list of those present at the May 25, 1999, 9:00 A.M. to 8:45 P.M. GAC meeting is printed in the executive minutes at www.noie.gov.au/projects/international/gac/meetings/mtg2/gac2min.htm [accessed January 19, 2003].

9. See note 8.

10. "ICANN Announces Dr. Paul Twomey as New President/CEO," ICANN, March 19, 2003, www.icann.org/announcements/announcement-19mar03.htm [accessed March 19, 2003].

11. For a more detailed description of my comments, see note 8.

12. See, for example, Ellen Romy, "Los Angeles, California, Government Advisory Committee Public Forum Informal, Unofficial, Incomplete and Unapproved Notes," *Domain Name Handbook*, November 2, 1999, www.domainhandbook.com/icann110299c.html [accessed January 19, 2003], and Jeri Clausing, "Internet Board Opens Chile Meeting Amid Protests," *New York Times*, August 24, 1999, www.nytimes.com/library/tech/99/08/cyber/articles/25domain.html [accessed January 19, 2003].

13. Under an exclusive agreement with the U.S. government, from 1992 until 1999 Virginia-based Network Solutions, Inc. (NSI), was the only authorized registrar (seller) of gTLDs .com, .org, and .net. NSI's role was twofold: It was responsible not only for registering new domain names but also for maintaining the registry, the database, of assigned names. While there could be many registrars of domain names, there is only one holder of the registry. When NSI's contract expired in 1998, the U.S. government transferred control of the three domains to ICANN to allow other companies to register the popular gTLDs and complete with NSI. ICANN also sought to assume control of the registry from NSI. After a year of negotiations, NSI recognized ICANN's authority, and the two parties managed to strike a deal. In 2000, web security company VeriSign Inc. acquired NSI. In 2001, the Department of Commerce approved a deal that allowed VeriSign to continue controlling the master list of the world's .com addresses through 2007 and .net addresses though 2005. For additional background, see, for example, Courtney Macavinta, "NSI Won't Sign On with ICANN," *News.com*, June 25, 1999, http://news.com.com/2100-1023-227699.html?legacy=cnet [accessed January 19, 2003]; "ICANN-NSI Registry Agreement," ICANN, November 10, 1999, www.icann.org/nsi/nsi-registry-agreement-04nov99.htm [accessed January 19, 2003]; Keith Perine, "Network Solutions and ICANN Make Peace," *The Industry Standard*, September 28, 1999, www.thestandard.com/article/0,1902,6631,00.html [accessed January 19, 2003]; and David McGuire, "ICANN Threatens to Take Away VeriSign's '.com' Privileges," *WashingtonPost.com*, September 4, 2002, www.washingtonpost.com/ac2/wp-dyn?pagename=article&node=&contentId=A34373-2002Sep3&notFound=true [accessed January 19, 2003].

14. Christine Winter, "Domain-Name Players Suit Up for Another Game; Number of Sites Registered Reaches into the Millions," *Sun-Sentinel* (Fort Lauderdale, Fla.), September 2, 2001, G1.

15. See Dot MD at www.dotmd.com [accessed January 19, 2003] and the MoldData registrar home page at www.nic.md [accessed January 19, 2003].

16. For more information about .cc, see eNIC at www.cc [accessed January 19, 2003].

~

CHAPTER NINE

China's .CN: Reaching Every Corner of the World

Erica Schlesinger Wass

It is not only small nations like Moldova and Niue that have chosen to market their domain endings to those outside the nation's borders. In fact, in a dramatic policy shift, China has begun to allow foreign companies to register domains under its country code top-level domain, .cn.

In this chapter, Erica Schlesinger Wass traces the Chinese name space from its restrictive roots to current open policies. In doing so, she shows that .cn is at the center of China's dreams of economic prosperity.

One of the first e-mails sent from China was titled "Crossing the Great Wall to Join the World." To encourage the huge number of Internet users from China and around the world to take part in China's Internet, those who govern China's country code top-level domain, .cn, have recently relaxed the rules to allow for domain name registrations from outside China. In doing so, they have once again shown China's willingness and desire to deal, economically, with the rest of the world.

Professors Qian Tian Bai and Qian Hua Lin were instrumental in creating China's network. They were in charge of the Internet project of the Chinese Academic Network (CANET), a scientific research project launched by the Beijing Municipal Computer Application Research Institute in 1986 in cooperation with Germany's Karlsruhe University. According to systems analyst Cindy Zheng, the owner and moderator of the chinanet mailing lists, at that time there was a lot of Chinese governmental fear about the Internet;

government policy was not supporting the development of the network infrastructure. Because of the lack of funding or government support to launch the network solely in China, Professors Qian and Qian connected with peers from Karlsruhe University with whom they had prior working experience.[1]

It was in late November 1990 that Qian Tian Bai registered the country code top-level domain .cn for China and became the first manager of the .cn name space. Qian Tian Bai, who died of a heart attack in 1998 at the age of fifty-three, has since been regarded as the father of the Internet in China. Since its delegation, Internet use and the registration of China's country code top-level domain, .cn, have skyrocketed.

Each of the early Chinese academic networks had one thing in common: None was directly connected to the Internet. At that time, the U.S. government forbade any socialist countries to access the Internet because the network contained, among other things, science and technology research.[2] In 1992, the Chinese government and the National Science Foundation discussed the possibility of connecting China to the Internet. However, China was informed that its access to the Internet would encounter political barriers because of the presence of U.S. government agencies on the Internet at that time.[3]

In early April 1994, delegates from China and the United States met in Washington, D.C., at the Sino-American Federation of Scientific and Technological Cooperation. On behalf of the Chinese government, Dr. Hu Qiheng, an academic and vice president of the Chinese Academy of Sciences, sought to persuade the National Science Foundation to allow China to link to the Internet. Meanwhile, throughout the early 1990s, major U.S. telecommunications companies were eager to advance into the Chinese marketplace, and the World Bank was funding major scientific and technological projects in China. These experiences educated both the Chinese and the Americans and influenced both governments to take more progressive stances; the appeal to the National Science Foundation had worked.[4]

Later that month, China connected to the Internet. Because all research and education funding came from the government and the Chinese funding structure did not promote sharing and collaborating among different branches of government, the Computer Network Information Center of the Chinese Academy of Sciences established the China Science and Technology Network (CSTNET). Although delegated in 1990, because there was no clear government policy and no money, the .cn domain was dormant until 1994. On May 21, 1994, however, both Professors Qian, with the help of Karlsruhe University, successfully established China's domestic server for the .cn domain on CSTNET. From then on, the .cn domain formally started operating within China, and the Computer Network Information Center of the Chinese Academy of Sciences started providing registration and resolution services for .cn.

The early policymaking authority for China's Internet infrastructure was the Ministry of Posts and Telecommunications (MPT), a government monopoly. Although MPT was an official organ of the State Council, which was responsible for China's postal and telecommunications services, in reality it was also policymaker, regulator, and operator. Within a few years, however, amidst bureaucratic wrangling among various ministries vying for control, power would change hands. Scholar Yu-Sun Jeong argues, "These trends suggest an institutional model of Communist policy-making that began with a clash of interests, followed by the creation of a coordinating system, and, finally, a merger of all concerned ministries."[5] These larger themes of Internet governance in China soon filtered down to affect the control over the domain name functions.

There is, however, an uneven geographical distribution of access. According to Professors Royal D. Colle and Liu Yonggong, almost 70 percent of all Internet users in China live in big cities, such as Beijing, Shanghai, and Guangzhou, and in the eastern coastal region. The thirteen provinces in western China have less than 1 percent of the country's Internet users, and vast parts of the country's western areas were not connected to the Internet in 2002. "This imbalance reflects regional disparity in general economic development and level of education."[6]

In February 1996, the Chinese government formally took charge of its Internet infrastructure when it issued the "Interim Regulations of the People's Republic of China on the Management of International Networking of Computer Information."[7] This document established the Information Working Group of the State Council, which would be the body to coordinate and regulate international computer networking, including the .cn domain.

Throughout 1997, the Information Working Group coordinated both the structure and the rules for .cn. The report "Provisional Measures for the Administration of Domain Name Registration on China's Internet Network" established the China Internet Network Information Center (CNNIC), which would be the nonprofit group responsible for the day-to-day administration and operation of .cn.[8] A second report, "Detailed Implementing Rules for the Registration of Domain Names on China's Internet," listed the restrictive rules for registering .cn domain names.[9]

As Zheng notes, "Internet development in China really showed how the Chinese government struggled to retain control and how unstoppable the Internet was. The Chinese government set a lot of rules along the way. The choice for the Chinese government was either to stop the Internet cold, or yield to it. I think that the rules reflect the system—the government wants to rule everyone and everything."[10]

Only entities that were registered with the government could register a .cn domain name; individuals were not eligible. Foreign entities seeking .cn domain names were required to have both their primary Domain Name Server in China and have a local branch or office. Zheng says that this was another control tactic. "The MPT—the government—owned all of the physical networks inside China. It wanted everyone on its networks to be non-virtual, so they could both control the flow of information and easily find any responsible people."

Registrants also had to register their names as third-level domains; the second-level name space reflected organizational domains, like .com.cn and .gov.cn, as well as regionally based domains, like .bj.cn for Beijing, .sh.cn for Shanghai, and .hk.cn for Hong Kong.

Where there were domain name disputes, the rules noted that "CNNIC shall not act as mediator, and the domain name registrant itself shall be responsible for handling the dispute and bear the legal liability." This was reflective of CNNIC's lack of both desire and legal authority to mediate disputes.

Run by the Chinese Academy of Sciences, CNNIC is under the authority of the Ministry of Information Industry (MII). The MII was a fusion and consolidation of each of the earlier ministries that had governed the Internet infrastructure.[11] From this point on, CNNIC has been under the leadership of both the Computer Network Information Center of the Chinese Academy of Sciences and the MII.

While in the late 1990s China's Internet had developed quickly, the percentage of .cn domain names registered by Chinese people declined significantly. In 1997, half the domain names registered by Chinese were under .cn; by 2000, that figure was less than 16 percent. This was troubling to ministry officials because they feared that a low .cn registration rate would lead to slower development of the Internet in China and less funding.[12] According to CNNIC Director Mao Wei, more than 700,000 domain names in China were registered not under .cn but under the generic top-level domains .com and .net. "This is not beneficial to the future of China's information security," Mao said.[13]

The importance of the Chinese Internet as a communications device is, in large part, based in history. In 1966, as Mao Tse-tung's power base eroded, he launched the proletarian Cultural Revolution to strengthen his position. "China's schools were closed and its youths were mobilized into Red Guard units, which attacked anything that seemed Western, Soviet or capitalist. The ideological fervor also hurt China's economy and threatened to spiral out of control."[14]

When the Cultural Revolution ended and China once again opened its doors, there was an extreme need to connect China with the rest of the world. Enhancing China's technological infrastructure became a top priority to achieve that goal. As Professors Cullen and Choy note, "Apart from the broad open door policy, the continuing shift towards a (socialist) market economy, state enterprise reform and the process of disengagement of the state from the detail of day-to-day living have also led to an increase in the demand for better communications."[15]

Politically at odds with itself, the open-door policy creates tension with the nation's political inclinations toward mass control and political management. Modernization remains a clear, widely supported goal. Because of its size, traditions, and especially its population, China correctly sees itself as an important world power. Technological backwardness over the past two centuries is one factor believed to have held China back from taking its rightful place in the world. Rectifying this technological lag is almost universally regarded as a fundamental good in China. The dangers that come with technological change—not least of all the political "pollution" of information flows—are widely recognized. Nevertheless, the need to change is still recognized as a fundamental requirement.[16]

While the Chinese government has been committed to strengthening its Internet infrastructure, it has at the same time strictly monitored and controlled content available on the Internet.[17] Communist Party of China authorities are sensitive about political content online and bar Chinese web surfers from seeing a wide range of foreign sites run by news organizations, human rights groups, and Chinese dissidents.[18] While these rules are geared toward visable external content within China, in September 2000 the State Council passed the Measures for Managing Internet Content Provision, which governed online content produced and published in China. The measures, a codification of existing regulations, govern who can own Internet businesses, what can be published on the Internet, and who oversees Internet businesses.[19]

It was not only the fear of censorship but also the cumbersome process that was seen as a barrier to registering under .cn. It took CNNIC officials time to process the registrations, each of which was required to be accompanied by extensive paperwork. As a result, the domain name approval process took about five days, as compared with a couple of hours for many other top-level domains. The cost of .cn domains was 300 yuan (U.S.$36), which, while only a couple of dollars more expensive than a yearly .com registration, was high enough to place a burden on Chinese workers, who have a low average yearly income.[20]

Registrants who also wanted to register their domains in the second level, which they can do under .com, could not under .cn's locality- and organizational-based second-level domains. An MII study found that about 90 percent of people wanted CNNIC to open the second-level domain to registrations.[21]

There were also language concerns. Despite the fact that many Chinese schoolchildren are now taught English as a second language, many Chinese Internet users and potential users do not speak English. The Latin-script, English-language character domain names were often as unfamiliar as the set of numbers in an IP (Internet Protocol) address. In fact, many popular Chinese websites do not use letters at all but, rather, numbers. One of China's most popular auction sites is "8848.net," 8848 being a play on the height in meters of Mount Everest and the lucky number 8, which sounds like "prosperity" in Chinese.[22] Still, despite using catchy names without an alphabet, Asian and other language speakers looked forward to having a domain name that represented their culture and their language scripts.

On September 30, 2002, CNNIC liberalized the registration policies for the .cn name space.[23] Since March 17, 2003, registrants have been able to register their domain names directly in the second level under .cn. Encouraging registrations, this change in policy has had a practical effect of lowering registration fees to 160 yuan (U.S.$19.35), half the earlier amount.[24] The change has been hailed as enhancing the competitive ability of .cn and thereby strengthening China's position in the world.[25]

The registration process has also been simplified, as applicants can register online and do not have to submit written applications and supporting documents. It takes only six hours for the process.[26] CNNIC also developed an extensive domain name resolution policy to arbitrate conflicts.[27]

Perhaps the most significant change was the removal of the requirement that applicants must be Chinese entities. Therefore, both Chinese and foreign entities now are permitted to register domain names directly under .cn.

The opening of the domain to foreign registrants, a political and an economic decision, reflects China's general willingness to engage economically with other nations. In November 2001, after fifteen years of negotiations, China was allowed to join the World Trade Organization (WTO). A WTO press release noted, "As a result of this negotiation, China has agreed to undertake a series of important commitments to open and liberalize its regime in order to better integrate in the world economy and offer a more predictable environment for trade and foreign investment in accordance with WTO rules."[28]

The entrance into the WTO has encouraged China to maintain its priorities and work toward creating and preserving economic ties with other nations. The recognition of domain names is just one technique being touted as China attracts $47 billion of foreign investment—more than any other developing country.[29]

NeuStar, Inc., a registrar that sells .cn addresses (and also runs .us and .biz), notes, "China's recent accession to the World Trade Organization (WTO) is proof that the Chinese economy is taking great strides toward accessibility. Now is an ideal time for companies to protect their brand identities in .cn, and to begin making inroads into the Chinese marketplace."[30] Richard Tindal, NeuStar's vice president for sales and marketing, has said, "With China's entrance into the World Trade Organization, international trade is also expected to accelerate. This initiative will enable companies worldwide to participate in China's growing economy via the Internet. We expect businesses in countries with strong trading relations with China, such as Korea, Hong Kong, Taiwan, Japan, the United States and Britain, to want a .cn presence."[31]

While the foreign registration of .cn domain names is encouraged, there are restrictions. To once again reconcile a history of strictly regulated Internet content with the desire to create an open domain name registration process, CNNIC has passed along its responsibilities as a registrar to private entities and now dedicates itself to monitoring and regulating the .cn name space. Basing its decisions on a rather lengthy list of registration guidelines, CNNIC and the registrars will decide which addresses are appropriate for the name space and will check the content of .cn sites, Mao said; decisions not favoring the registrant can then be appealed to the MII.[32]

The change in rules has managed to achieve the goal of increasing the use of .cn. In the three months after the new rules were announced, the number of domains registered under .cn continually increased.[33] With just over 56 million homes in China connected to the Internet—only 5 percent—China already has the second-largest population of Internet users, behind the United States.[34] The words of that early e-mail are prophetic. Through the use of its country code top-level domain, China has indeed gone beyond the Great Wall and is managing to reach every corner of the world.

Notes

1. Cindy Zheng, e-mails to author, March 13, 2003; the chinanet e-mailing lists provide for discussion and information exchange on topics related directly to China networking. See www.sdsc.edu/~zhengc/chinanet.html [accessed March 19, 2003]. For further background on Ms. Zheng's work with Chinese Internet networking, see www.sdsc.edu/~zhengc/china.html [accessed March 12, 2003].

2. "Evolution of Internet in China," CNNIC, www.cnnic.net.cn/evolution.shtml [accessed March 12, 2003].

3. "China's Internet Development Timeline," ChinaOnline, www.chinaonline.com/issues/internet_policy/c9101571.asp [accessed March 12, 2003].

4. Interview with Cindy Zheng (see note 1).

5. Yousun Chung, "Anatomy of the Decision-Making Process in China: (De) Concentration of the Internet Industry," Seoul National University thesis, 2002, http://sias.snu.ac.kr/i/i-thesis/i-0202thesis/ysjeong.pdf [accessed March 20, 2003].

6. Royal D. Colle and Liu Yonggong, "ICT Capacity-Building for Development and Poverty Alleviation: Enhancing the Role of Agricultural Universities in China," October 2002, http://ip.cals.cornell.edu/commdev/documents/ictpaper-china.doc [accessed March 12, 2003].

7. "Interim Regulations of the People's Republic of China on the Management of International Networking of Computer Information," http://product.chinawe.com/cgi-bin/lawdetail.pl?LawID=568 [accessed May 17, 2003].

8. "Provisional Administrative Rules for Registration of Domain Names on China's Internet," CNNIC, May 1997, www.cnnic.net.cn/doc/e-3.shtml [accessed March 12, 2003].

9. "Detailed Implementation Rules for Registration of Domain Names on China's Internet" CNNIC, June 1997, www.cnnic.net.cn/doc/e-4.shtml [accessed March 12, 2003].

10. Zheng interview.

11. See note 5.

12. Fu Jing, "More '.cn' to Be Seen in Domain Name," *ChinaDaily.com.cn*, August 17, 2002, www1.chinadaily.com.cn/cndy/2002-08-17/82510.html [accessed March 12, 2003].

13. Fu Jing, "New Regulation Eases Domain Access," *ChinaDaily.com.cn*, December 13, 2002, www1.chinadaily.com.cn/cndy/2002-12-13/97725.html [accessed March 12, 2003].

14. "Visions of China: The Red Giant," *CNN.com*, 1999, www.cnn.com/SPECIAL/1999/china.50/red.giant [accessed March 12, 2003].

15. Richard Cullen and Pinky D. W. Choy, "The Internet in China," *Columbia Journal of Asian Law* 13, no. 1 (Spring):107–8.

16. See note 15.

17. See, for example, Benjamin Edelman and Jonathan Zittrain, "Empirical Analysis of Internet Filtering in China," Berkman Center for Internet and Society, Harvard Law School, December 2002, http://cyber.law.harvard.edu/filtering/china [accessed March 12, 2003].

18. "China Beefs Up Biz with Dot-Cn," Associated Press on Wired.com, October 31, 2003, www.wired.com/news/politics/0,1283,56124,00.html [accessed March 12, 2003]; see also Michael S. Chase and James C. Mulvenon, "You've Got Dissent! Chinese Dissident Use of the Internet and Beijing's Counter-Strategies," RAND, 2002, www.rand.org/publications/MR/MR1543 [accessed March 12, 2003]; Patrick Di Justo, "Does the End Justify the Means?" Wired News, March 18, 2003, www.wired.com/news/politics/0,1283,58082,00.html [accessed March 20, 2003].

19. "China's New Internet Law," Digital Freedom Network, October 6, 2000, www.dfn.org/voices/china/netreg-0010txt.htm [accessed March 13, 2003].

20. See note 13.

21. See Qian Hualin, "Speech Commemorating Opening of .cn Second-Level Name Space," March 17, 2003, www.cnnic.cn/ruler/0317_3.shtml [accessed March 20, 2003]; see also ".cn News," www.cnnic.net.cn/registration/newslist.shtml [accessed March 20, 2003].

22. "Cyber-Squatting Fears Grow," BBC News, November 14, 2000, http://news. bbc.co.uk/hi/english/business/newsid_1023000/1023191.stm [accessed March 13, 2003].

23. See "China Internet Domain Name Regulations," CNNIC, September 30, 2002, www.cnnic.net.cn/doc/e-8.shtml [accessed March 12, 2003]; see also "China Revamps Internet Domain Name System," Perkins Coie LLP, www.perkinscoie.com/resource/ intldocs/revamp_dns.htm [accessed March 12, 2003].

24. See note 21.

25. See note 21.

26. Dr. Mao Wei, e-mail to author, March 20, 2003.

27. "CNNIC Domain Name Dispute Resolution Policy," CNNIC, September 30, 2002, www.cnnic.net.cn/doc/e-10.shtml [accessed March 12, 2003]; CNNIC adopted a modified version of the Uniform Dispute Resolution Policy; see also, for example, Scott Donahey, "The New Dispute Resolution Procedures for .cn," March 3, 2003, www.itu.int/itudoc/itu-t/workshop/cctld/cctld015.pdf [accessed March 12, 2003].

28. "WTO Ministerial Conference Approves China's Accession," WTO press release, November 10, 2001, www.wto.org/english/news_e/pres01_e/pr252_e.htm [accessed March 12, 2003].

29. Ambassador Serigo Marchi, "The World Trade Organization: From Doha and Beyond, Notes for an Address to the Central Party School of China" May 24, 2002, www.wto.org/english/news_e/news02_e/china_accession_24may02_e.doc [accessed March 20, 2003].

30. NeuStar.com.cn home page at http://neustar.com.cn/whycn/index.html [accessed March 12, 2003].

31. Carolyn Ong, "Foreigners Set for .CN Swoop; Mainland Braces for Flood of Demand When It Opens the Domain Name Market in Dec.," *South China Morning Post*, October 30, 2002, 12.

32. As of the writing of this chapter, Dr. Mao did not know of any websites that had been turned down because of registration policies. Article 19 of the China Internet Domain Name Regulations says, "Any of the following contents shall not be included in any domain name registered and used by any organization or individual: 1. Those that are against the basic principles prescribed in the Constitution; 2. Those that jeopardize national security, leak state secrets, intend to overturn the government, or disrupt of state integrity; 3. Those that harm national honor and national interests; 4. Those that instigate hostility or discrimination between different nationalities, or disrupt the national solidarity; 5. Those that violate the state religion policies or propagate cult and feudal superstition; 6. Those that spread rumors, disturb public order or disrupt social stability; 7. Those that spread pornography, obscenity, gambling, violence, homicide, terror or instigate crimes; 8. Those that insult, libel against others and infringe other people's legal rights and interests; or 9. Other contents prohibited in laws, rules and administrative regulations"; see "China Internet Domain Name Regulations," CNNIC, September 30, 2002, www.cnnic.net.cn/ruler/20.shtml [accessed March 19, 2003].

33. "Domain Names Registered under .CN," CNNIC, www.cnnic.net.cn/
e-domain.shtml [accessed March 12, 2003].

34. "Nielsen/Netratings Finds China Has the World's Second Largest At-Home
Internet Population," Nielsen/Netratings, April 22, 2002, www.nielsen-netratings.
com/pr/pr_020422_eratings.pdf [accessed March 12, 2003].

~

CHAPTER TEN

Swaziland's .SZ: Virtual Symbols of Swaziland's National Aspirations and Character

Paiki Muswazi

Regardless of whether a nation is highly developed or in the process of developing, the lure of communication and e-commerce is too strong to ignore. While some nations have marketed their country code top-level domains (ccTLDs) to the world to raise national capital, others, like the southern African Kingdom of Swaziland, have turned inward and used their ccTLDs to promote both a national development scheme and a global awareness of their culture.

In this chapter, Paiki Muswazi, a special collections librarian at the University of Swaziland who has written extensively about the social implications of the Internet as it applies to developing countries like Swaziland, introduces us to the .sz name space and the sites that use it to attain a national vision.

The Kingdom of Swaziland is a small landlocked country in southern Africa, located between Mozambique and South Africa. Almost completely surrounded by South Africa, Swaziland was a British colony until 1968, when it gained independence. SiSwati and English are the official languages of the Swazi people. Swaziland has an estimated population of one million, 70 percent of whom live in rural areas and are supported by subsistence farming.[1] While the United Nations Development Program (UNDP) classifies Swaziland as a medium human development country and the World Bank classifies it as a lower-middle-income country, the government contests these categorizations and, based on socioeconomic realities, argues that it is overrated.

Besides the controversy surrounding its development status, its monarchical government under King Mswati III, nonparty political system, and strong cultural traditions make Swaziland distinctive. The Swazi monarchy is one of the oldest on the African continent; it boasts a deeply entrenched and resilient oral and expressive culture, which, to a large extent, has survived the ravages of colonialism and managed to coexist with alien cultural influences.

Emerging socioeconomic challenges and democratic waves sweeping across Africa have exerted pressure on the fabric of Swazi society. Swaziland has responded by initiating constitutional review and long-range strategic planning processes. Of particular interest was the issuance in 1999 of the National Development Strategy (NDS), which articulated the national vision: "By the year 2022, the Kingdom of Swaziland will be in the top ten percent of the medium human development group of countries founded on sustainable economic development, social justice and political stability."[2]

The NDS acknowledges the importance of information and knowledge in the attainment of national aspirations. In fact, the NDS rollout processes coincided with the adoption of the Internet and its unprecedented effects on information transfer and sharing between communities and across international borders.

The social, political, and economic potential of the Internet in developing nations is, by its very nature, a subject of sustained debate. Many argue that it imparts the ability to leapfrog decades of development and accelerate the attainment of prosperity, that it may result in the effacement of indigenous cultures, and that it can make ubiquity of access to information and knowledge a reality for the poor.[3]

Of course, these arguments are generalizations. In specific contexts, there are multiple challenges. Mike Jensen, a South African information systems consultant, succinctly notes that the process of advancing Internet use in Africa must be tailored to such specific conditions as generally low income levels, limited formal business activity, the great importance of the rural population and small producers, and the shared use of Internet accounts.[4]

In Swaziland, full Internet access was introduced in early 1996. The estimated average number of Internet users, that is, the increasingly information and knowledge empowered, is just over 6,500, which represents 0.64 percent of the total population; 40 to 60 percent of the users are eighteen to twenty-nine years old and evenly represent the sexes.[5] As often occurs in other developing nations, the introduction of the Internet was propelled by the cooperative efforts between public institutions, the private sector, and international development agencies. The Swaziland Posts and Telecommunications Corporation, a public enterprise that is responsible to the Ministry of Tourism and Communications, provided the communications backbone. It laid a fiber-optic line that stretched through the thirty-five-kilometer (twenty-four-mile) Manzini, Matsapha, Ezulwini, and Mbabane industrial and commercial corridor that connected to the South African communications network. Connectivity was slow and excluded the outlying areas. As a result, for the 70 percent of Swazis in the remote and outlying rural areas, universal access to information was a pipe dream.

Still, in Swaziland, the potential of the Internet has not gone unnoticed. The attention has resulted in the country's registration and occupation of the .sz name space on the Internet. For many stakeholders, .sz is an increasingly focal point in the pursuit of the ideals enshrined in the national vision.

The Swaziland Internet Service Provider Association coordinates domain registration under the top-level country code domain, .sz, and charges a nominal administrative service fee of E200 (U.S.$20) per year.[6] A national information and communication technology committee with representatives from the education, information, communication, and information technology sectors is formulating policies and legislation to, inter alia, regulate Internet service provision. Basically, the thrust in Swaziland is creating and nurturing conditions that support Internet development.

The usage of the .sz name space can be divided into four broad categories: 1) e-commerce; 2) communication of the national vision, strategies, priorities, and programs; 3) cultural promotion, preservation, and commercialization; and 4) social and political regulation.

E-commerce, the harnessing of the Internet for marketing and trading purposes, is considered an engine of socioeconomic growth. In fact, the relative ease with which Swaziland embraced the Internet is the result of the Internet's ability to provide a means to access the national and global marketplace. Perhaps one of the most predominant uses of .sz is the marketing of Swaziland goods and services, which run the gamut from traditional crafts, local books, polyester, cotton, glass, sugar, citrus fruits, pineapples, cotton, and maize to accounting, advertising, financial, insurance, tourism, medical, and media and communications services. Companies and organizations extensively use the .sz name space to distribute e-catalogs and mount Internet displays and exhibitions to market their products.[7]

Beyond online advertising, real-time online transactions in the .sz name space are minimal. The lack of watertight security and identification standards dissuades banks, retailers, consumers, and many others from fully exploiting the trade opportunities offered by the Internet.

While .sz is unmistakably a tool for e-commerce, the paradox is that it is also a stark reminder of the harshness of the commerce and industry terrain in Swaziland. Often links to commerce sites are broken, and despite advances, it is sobering to think that only the few advantaged and high-income 0.64 percent of the population has access to e-commerce services.

Equally consoling, however, is the vast exposure to a worldwide consumer base that ultimately benefits the Swazi economy and society. Describing its Internet advertising service, *The Guardian of Swaziland* observes that it has had visitors from more than thirty countries.[8] On balance, .sz not only sharpens class differences in Swazi society but also connects the larger socioeconomic infrastructure to the global commercial market.

The government of the Kingdom of Swaziland also uses .sz to communicate and attain the national vision enunciated in the NDS. Over and above e-commerce, the .sz name space includes information on such national strategies and policies as creating a sustainable national budget and a realistic monetary policy to increase investor confidence, economic empowerment, appropriate education and training, agricultural development covering commercialization of the subsistence sector, efficient water resource management and usage, rational land allocation and usage, research and development, and environmental management.[9] Government, public enterprises, and other organizations also use .sz to apprise the public on the direction of the vision over time.[10] By providing a means to readily juxtapose information on the government's official position against independent observations on actual practice, .sz serves to present balanced and objective views on Swaziland's economic performance.

The Enterprise Trust Fund and Small Enterprise Development Company websites are populated with information, guidelines, and assistance available to indigenous small and medium businesses in Swaziland.[11] In this instance, .sz informs and educates indigenous communities and the larger public on the enabling institutional structures servicing the economic empowerment national strategy. It is thereby serving as an awareness-raising tool.

Swaziland's ongoing human resources development reforms entail the provision of skills relevant to national needs. In this regard, institutions like Mananga and the University of Swaziland (UNISWA) use the .sz name space to publicize a wide range of relevant course offerings tailored to meet that need.[12]

The fact that UNISWA is reported to have the highest Internet traffic in Swaziland underscores the educational utility of the technology. In many respects, .sz is an educational tool and a meeting place between training service providers and service consumers. At the macro level, it provides a medium for advertising national skills development incentives to a wider audience. Thus, when the Swaziland Investment Promotion Authority announces a 150 percent rebate on training of local personnel to international investors on its website,[13] it is clearly identifying human resources development as a national priority area in Swaziland.

Agricultural development is also key to the attainment of the NDS vision. Both government and public enterprises use the .sz name space to provide insight into the programs that translate the vision into reality.[14] At the other end of the scale, .sz is used to market agricultural products and services as well as to give information on export and marketing structures.[15]

The inseparable interrelationship between agriculture, weather conditions, and Swazi national life has been expressed by King Mswati III. In a speech, he urges the nation to "pray for continued rain so that good harvest may be expected."[16] In this context, the Swaziland Meteorological Service uses .sz to update the nation and beyond on weather and climate conditions to facilitate, inter alia, agricultural planning.[17] The speech and the weather updates give insight to the influence of natural phenomena on the rhythm of Swazi national life and, by extension, the Swazi national psyche in general. The diversity and depth of agricultural information at the .sz name space is commensurate with the national significance attached to the sector. To that extent, .sz is a mirror of Swaziland's priorities and preoccupations.

The NDS also highlights the value placed on evidence-based development. It encourages research, dissemination, and application of research results. The .sz domain is used for hosting information valuable to research and dissemination of research results for use in addressing topical issues relevant to Swaziland. Indeed, from 1999 to 2002, there was an increase in the volume of research information in the .sz name space. Though still on a relatively small scale and perhaps reflecting the volume of research that could possibly be generated by small developing nations like Swaziland, .sz provides a medium for publicizing agricultural, educational, and other research results.[18]

Furthermore, the .sz name space facilitates national and international information and knowledge sharing by providing a forum for announcing conferences and proceedings. For example, the UNISWA conferences site periodically announces conference events and paper presentations on national burning issues, such as the HIV/AIDS conference program.[19] The domain has, therefore, become a window to national concerns and collective responses.

In addition to using .sz to aid the alleviation of the nation's social problems, the Swaziland government and other public organizations also use .sz to demonstrate Swaziland's national environmental consciousness. The nation is focused on sustainable human and social development and providing policy guidance on environmental management issues.[20]

By and large, the diversity of authoritative information and knowledge accessible at .sz makes the domain a powerful educational tool promoting understanding of Swaziland and its aspirations. It is a communication bridge between government and the citizenry on the one hand and the Swazi nation and the world on the other.

Increasingly, .sz is serving as the national memory, recording the collective ideals, programs, priorities, achievements, and failures of Swaziland. However, a discussion of .sz cannot be considered complete without analyzing the cultural context that makes Swaziland distinctive.

Among many commentators, Balam Nyeko, a professor of history at the University of Swaziland, observed that Swaziland has tended to retain and cherish many of its precolonial traditions.[21] In the predominantly oral Swazi society, print and mass media are harnessed to serve traditional cultural ends. Whether the Internet will alter the cultural balance of power in Swaziland is a matter of conjecture. What is clear is that information on what could be called the pillars of Swazi culture is accessible in the .sz name space.

As the centerpiece of Swazi national consciousness, culture is as symbolic in the information and knowledge era powered by the Internet as it was traditionally. There could be no better demonstration of this than King Mswati III's speech, which at the outset stated, "I should like to commend the nation for the very high attendance at traditional and cultural events throughout the year. This is a clear indication of the importance we attach to this area of national life and that new generations are strongly committed to preserving our culture and heritage."[22]

The Swaziland National Trust Commission (SNTC) is vested with the institutional responsibility to promote and preserve Swazi culture in all its forms, including print, artifacts, oral, and electronic. Consistent with historical trends, the English language is harnessed within .sz to depict, by words and images, major traditional ceremonies, dance, dress, and customs. These include the *Incwala* (Kingship Ceremony), the *Umhlanga* (Reed Dance), the *Sibhaca* (a vigorous foot dance performed by teams of men), and traditional attire. The .sz name space is also the home to sites that describe a selection of SiSwati language words at the core of acceptable social etiquette as well as traditional foods that constitute the typical Swazi staple diet.[23]

The SNTC and the Ministry of Tourism and Communications recognize culture as one of Swaziland's major tourism showcases. In this respect, the .sz name space is increasingly used to publicize cultural resources to attract the worldwide tourist market to generate much-needed revenue. The tariffs posted online attest to the role of .sz in the commercialization of Swazi culture.[24]

Overall, the .sz Internet name space serves as a tool for educating the Swazi public and the world on Swazi culture; promoting and preserving Swazi culture for posterity; providing a sense of national cultural pride, identity, and fulfillment; symbolizing national consciousness; commercializing cultural resources; and contributing to the emergence of a new form of a globally connected civilization on the Internet-shared space, where different cultures coexist without terrestrial hindrances.

It appears that culture resources within .sz can only improve, thereby attracting the attention of a competitive global tourist market and at the same time buttressing the legendary buoyancy that Swazi culture has traditionally commanded. The use of multimedia technology and the predictions that World Resources Institute Chief Information Officer Allen L. Hammond makes on the potential of voice recognition software to provide access to illiterate people hold promise for Swaziland's indigenous oral culture.[25]

With the responsible institutional structures embracing the culture propagation and preservation opportunities offered by the .sz name space, the prospect of the information and knowledge age destroying the Swazi culture monument appears remote, even considering an influx of powerful outside forces. While a key indicator of many cultures is fierce political debate, political parties are legally banned in Swaziland. Similarly, publications carrying views radically contrary to officially acceptable mainstream thinking are banned under the Proscribed Publications Act of 1968. Political associations, pressure groups, and quasi-political bodies—such as the People's United Democratic Movement (PUDEMO), Swaziland Democratic Alliance (SDA), Swaziland Federation of Trade Unions (SFTU), Swaziland National Association of Teachers, Swaziland National Association of Civil Servants, and student bodies—play an opposition role, but it is not legally permissible for them to hold political meetings.

The constitutional reform process seeks to accommodate the wishes of all Swazi people, but, until it is finalized, the proscriptive regulations are in force. These democratic tensions and contradictions have seen the banning and unbanning of the independent *Guardian of Swaziland* newspaper and the *Nation Magazine* in 2001, the holding of a political rally in neighboring South Africa in 2000, and the detention and trial of PUDEMO's president in 2002.[26]

The availability of varying opinions on the Internet provides a sense of perspective to the social and political forces influencing the Swaziland sociopolitical edifice. There are essentially three forces: the official, the independent, and the ultrademocratic. Internet publications within and outside the .sz name space project the dimensions of the polarization. Official government views can be read at *Swaziland Today* and *The Swazi Observer*.[27] Legally acceptable independent views, though sometimes considered controversial and subject to official censure, are accessible at *The Times of Swaziland* and *The Guardian of Swaziland*.[28] Despite the range of materials available within .sz, the name space excludes views that, officially, are beyond the legal limits. Those with these views often take refuge at sites outside .sz.[29]

Although there are no specific statutory Internet regulations and government has no control over what Internet Service Providers (ISPs) publish, the general proscriptive legal framework exerts some influence on the information hosted within .sz. The domain lies in the intellectual property realm for which the Swazi state has vested interests and therefore tends to operate within the limits of existing laws. Arguably, therefore, it serves to regulate freedom of expression. The envisaged establishment of a government ISP will consolidate control of what is published, especially information about the government. However, at least in the Swazi politicocultural context, by providing a forum for the expression of what is considered unacceptable extremist dissent, the virtual Internet space surrounding .sz counterbalances territorial legal and official controls on social and political discourse. Thus, if the information within .sz projects a relatively homogeneous and tolerant political dispensation, the dissenting voices within the environs of .sz betray the underlying schisms pervading Swazi society.

The collaborative efforts of the public and private sectors and international development cooperation agencies, coupled with relatively affordable costs, stimulated Internet development in the Kingdom of Swaziland. It is important to observe that, generally, print information on Swaziland is not readily available, especially outside Swaziland; .sz is increasingly filling this lacuna, regardless of location, thereby promoting universal understanding of a country that, because of its small size, may not be well known in the global arena.

Advertently or inadvertently, .sz has become a tool for marketing Swazi goods and services; communicating between the government and the citizenry and the Swazi nation and the world; disseminating and sharing information and knowledge for use in dealing with national topical issues, education and training, cultural promotion, preservation and commercialization, and social and political regulation; nurturing a sense of national consciousness, pride, and identity; and sharpening class differentiation in Swazi society.

Emerging technologies and the lure of tourism revenue have the potential to deepen the indigenous flavor of .sz and to consolidate its culture content. By serving as a repository of information from government, the private sector, public enterprises, pressure groups, and individuals and associations, .sz reflects the synergies, tensions, and contradictions defining Swaziland's national character. Although relatively underutilized, the .sz name space is an icon of Swaziland's electronic heritage.

Notes

1. Swaziland Human Development Forum, *Swaziland Human Development Report 2000* (Mbabane, Swaziland: United Nations Development Program, 2001), 22.
2. Swaziland Ministry of Economic Planning and Development, *National Development Strategy: Vision 2022: Key Macro and Sectoral Strategies* (Mbabane, Swaziland: The Ministry, 1999), www.ecs.co.sz/nds [accessed February 15, 2003].

3. Mark Malloch Brown, "ICT for Development: A New Vision," *Cooperation South* 1 (2001): 2–4.

4. Mike Jensen, "Afriboxes, Telecenters, Cybercafes: ICT in Africa," *Cooperation South* 1 (2001): 97.

5. AfricaOnline.com Audience Profile, at www.africaonline.com/site/Articles/1,10,498.jsp [accessed February 15, 2003].

6. "E" is the abbreviation for "Emalangeni," which is the plural of "Lilangeni," the Swazi currency. For registration rules and procedures, see "Application to Establish a Sub-Domain within the SZ Namespace of the Internet, 2002," Swaziland ISP Association, SZ Top-Level Domain Registration Office, www.sispa.org.sz/Domreg [accessed February 15, 2003].

7. For example, numerous companies advertise their products at Swazi.com at www.realnet.co.sz and Africa Online at www.africaonline.co.sz/commerce. See also the Swaziland Royal Insurance Corporation at www.sric.sz, Ngwenya Glass at www.ngwenyaglass.co.sz, and other arts-and-crafts sites available at www.mintour.gov.sz/royalexperience/art.html [all accessed February 15, 2003].

8. See "Advertising at the Guardian," www.theguardian.co.sz/advertising.html [accessed May 27, 2002]; subsequently, the publication of *The Guardian of Swaziland* was temporarily suspended until adequate funding could be sourced.

9. For details, see "The Ministry of Economic Planning and Development's National Development Strategy," www.ecs.co.sz/nds [accessed February 15, 2003], and "Swazi National Policies, Action Plans and Strategies," www.ecs.co.sz/env_policies.htm [accessed February 15, 2003].

10. Swazi.com at www.realnet.co.sz [accessed February 15, 2003] provides the overview of the government budget and related policy initiatives such as the Public Sector Management Program. In addition, the 2001 budget speech at www.swazinews.co.sz/budget/budget_2001.htm [accessed February 15, 2003] notes the country's recurring fiscal deficits and investment vicissitudes. The Swaziland Investment Promotion Authority at www.sipa.org.sz/onestopshop.html [accessed February 15, 2003] portrays the country's investor-friendly climate, including investment guidelines and assistance available to investors. On the other hand, the Central Bank of Swaziland's 2001 monetary policy at www.centralbank.sz/cbs_policy.html [accessed February 15, 2003] observes increased unemployment and a slowdown in investment, and criticizes public overexpenditure; thus, "continuous escalation of current expenditure mainly on salaries whilst the revenue base is not improved is a reflection of government's inability to adhere to sound public finance policies."

11. See the Enterprise Trust Fund at www.etf.co.sz [accessed February 15, 2003], and the Small Enterprises Development Company at www.business-Swaziland.com/sedco [accessed February 15, 2003].

12. See Small and Micro Enterprise Management at www.mananga.sz/small_and_micro_enterprise.html, management of irrigation projects at www.mananga.sz/irrigation_projects.html, the 2002 calendar of courses at www.mananga.sz/course_outlines.html, and the bachelor of science in agriculture at www.uniswa.sz/agriculture/bsc_agric.html [all accessed February 15, 2003].

13. "One Stop Shop: Meeting the Investor," Swaziland Investment Promotion Authority, www.sipa.org.sz [accessed February 15, 2003].

14. Exemplary sites in this regard are Usuthu smallholder irrigation project at www.ecs.co.sz/projects_lowerusuthu_backgnd.htm, Phase 2: Komati Downstream Development Project at www.skpe.co.sz/sidvwashini.html, and Maguga Dam at www.ecs.co.sz/projects_magugadam.htm [all accessed February 15, 2003].

15. See the Ministry of Tourism and Communications at www.mintour.gov.sz/ royalexperience/agriculture.html, Swaziland Internet Directory at www.directory.sz/ internet/cat.cgi?agric, and Swaziland Investment Promotion Authority at www.sipa. org.sz/horticulture.html [all accessed February 15, 2003].

16. The entire speech is accessible through Swazi.com at www.Swazi.com/ government/speeches/parliament_2002.html [accessed February 15, 2003].

17. The weather updates are accessible via the National Meteorological Service at www.swazimet.gov.sz/Home.html [accessed February 15, 2003].

18. Notable sites serving this purpose include Research at UNISWA at www. uniswa.sz/research, publications by Dr. Cisco Magagula at www.realnet.co.sz/ide/ cisco_full_publications.htm, and UNISWA's online public access catalog at http:// library.uniswa.sz [all accessed February 15, 2003].

19. Available at www.uniswa.sz/conference/prov.html [accessed February 15, 2003].

20. See the Swaziland Environmental Action Plan at www.ecs.co.sz/seap/projects_ seap_vol2_chapter3c.htm [accessed February 15, 2003].

21. Balam Nyeko, *Swaziland* (Oxford: Clio Press, 1982).

22. The full speech is available at www.swazi.com/government/speeches/ parliament_2002.html [accessed February 15, 2003].

23. For sites promoting and preserving Swazi culture see, for example, SNTC cultural resources at www.sntc.org.sz/cultural/cultural.html, lifestyle and culture at www. mintour.gov.sz/royalexperience/lifestyle.html, Mantenga Cultural Village at www.sntc. org.sz/cultural/mantvill.html, Reilly's Rock Hilltop Lodge at www.biggame.co.sz/rr_ culture.html, and Swazi Trails at www.swazitrails.co.sz/strails.html [all accessed February 15, 2003].

24. See Swaziland National Trust Commission at www.sntc.org.sz/tourism/tariffs. html [accessed February 15, 2003].

25. Allen L. Hammond, "Digitally Empowered Development," *Cooperation South* 1 (2001): 7–8.

26. Swaziland, *Proscribed Publications Legal Notice No. 69 of 2001*, proscribed the two publications with effect from May 4, 2001; Swaziland, *Decree No. 2 of 2001*, endorsed by King Mswati III on June 22, 2001, among other things, clarified that government shall not be required to explain reasons for proscription and that no legal proceedings may be instituted in relation to such proscription; and Swaziland, *Decree No. 3 of 2001*, endorsed by King Mswati III on July 24, 2001, repealed *Decree No. 2 of 2001*, following public appeals.

27. See *Swaziland Today* at www.swazi.com/government/sgt-nl.html [accessed February 15, 2003], and *The Swazi Observer* at www.observer.org.sz [accessed February 15, 2003].

28. See *The Times of Swaziland* at www.times.co.sz, and *The Guardian of Swaziland* at http://theguardian.co.sz . If you have difficulty accessing *The Guardian of Swaziland* website, refer to explanatory notes in note 8.

29. See, for example, SDA, SFTU, and PUDEMO, "Mpumalanga Declaration," November 5, 2000, www.cosatu.org.za/sftu/mpdec.htm [accessed February 15, 2003]; "Statement from PUDEMO International Office," March 22, 1996, www. hartford-hwp.com/archives/37/067.html [accessed February 15, 2003]; "Activists Picket for Democracy in Swaziland," February 1, 2002, www.sacp.org.za/pr/2002/ pr0201.html [accessed February 15, 2003]; and "Swaziland: PUDEMO's Masuku Goes on Trial Jan. 24," December 27, 2001, www.africaonline.com/site/Articles/ 1,3,44290.jsp [accessed February 15, 2003].

~

CHAPTER ELEVEN

The United States' .US:
Striving for the American Dream

Erica Schlesinger Wass

Just as many people recognize that .uk is the country code top-level domain (ccTLD) for the United Kingdom and that .jp is the code for Japan, many people also believe that the code for the United States is .com.

In this chapter, Erica Schlesinger Wass introduces .us—the ccTLD for the United States. As the oldest ccTLD, .us has evolved to more consistently reflect the diversity of American identities and priorities.

Until 2002, there were fewer than 15,000 sites registered under .us, most of which were registered by public libraries and primary schools.[1] For years, the .us name space was underutilized because of indecision over its hierarchical structure, controversy over its purpose, and the ease and accessibility of its mighty counterpart, .com. In 2002, however, the .us regulations were revamped, governance of the domain was transferred to a private commercial entity, and .us addresses were marketed to those seeking a more patriotic Internet presence.

The confusion over the true United States domain suffix is well documented. In December 2002, the Federal Trade Commission settled a dispute with several domain name sellers who were selling domains ending in .usa, an unauthorized ending that has no practical use on the Internet.[2] After September 11, 2001, these companies launched a spam e-mail campaign; with a subject line reading, "Be Patriotic! Register .USA Domains," the e-mail connected consumers to a website where they were offered a .usa domain name for $59. In the settlement, the offending companies agreed to repay customers as much as $300,000; this would translate to more than 5,000 domains registered in the nonexistent name space.

Perhaps .usa would have been more popular than the .us ending; after all, Americans do not chant "U-S" at international sporting events but "U-S-A." Yet, despite the appeal, because of the strict guidelines for top-level domains (TLDs), a three-lettered country code is simply not possible. With designations for educational institutions (.edu) and government offices (.gov), for example, the three-lettered, generic top-level domains (gTLDs) were based not on geography but on organization.[3] The two-letter country code top-level domains (ccTLDs), which were founded on national lines, were not customizable because, for the most part, they were taken straight from a preestablished list of recognized "country names."[4] As a result, there was not and likely never will be room for .usa in the domain name space. But what about .us?

While .us was the first ccTLD to be delegated, it developed alongside the other country codes.[5] In February 1985, Dr. Jon Postel at the Information Sciences Institute of the University of Southern California (USC-ISI) became the administrator of .us in addition to his larger domain name duties as the Internet Assigned Numbers Authority (IANA). It was he who ultimately had to consider the structure of the .us domain name space and its registration rules.

The most visible choice that he made for the .us domain was the structure of the domain names. Whereas some ccTLDs, like Chile's .cl and Germany's .de, allowed registrations directly under their codes and others required registration under any of a number of second-level domains, like .co.uk for British companies, the hierarchical structure of .us was different. The multilevel names under .us were based not on organization but on political geography.

Reading the domain name from right to left, the domain names honed in on the registrant like the zoom of a camera, from most general to most specific. So the first level was .us, the second level was the state abbreviation, the third level was the city or county name, the fourth level was the organization name, and so on. The Ford Motor Company's corporate site, for example, would have had a .us site at "www.ford.dearborn.mi.us."

Postel chose this type of structure to prevent confusion and ensure availability. Because gTLDs like .com and .edu were already popular among domain name registrants, he did not want to include similar identifiers in the .us name space. While other ccTLDs adopted second-level domains, like .co and .org, that were similar to the gTLDs, Postel did not want users to be confused by the use of both .com and .com.us addresses.

In addition, because the political geography domains were so specific, there was little chance that the space would run out of names, which was a constant concern in the .com name space. "Maybe the plan for the US Domain is overkill on growth planning, but there has never been over-planning for growth yet," Postel wrote in RFC 1480, the document outlining the .us domain.

In the early days of .us, American organizations had registered sites primarily in the .edu and .com name spaces. As a result, little use was initially made of the .us domain. The first expansion of the domain was the result of the creation of categories of sites that were left out by the gTLDs.

For example, until recently, the rules of .edu required that registrants be four-year colleges and universities.[6] Two-year colleges and other educational institutions were prohibited from registering .edu domains. Using the domain name structure <schoolname>.cc.<state>.us, community colleges gained a familiar structure on the Internet. Public primary schools were free to register domains under <schoolname>.k12.<state>.us. The .us name space, however, allowed specialized names not only for community colleges and primary schools but also for a multitude of state and local government agencies.

The New York State website address, for example, is www.state.ny.us. The New York State Office of the Attorney General's website is, more specifically, at www.oag.state.ny.us. Similarly, the official New York State tourism board, called I Love NY, is located at www.iloveny.state.ny.us. The hierarchy was useful for this governmental purpose because it allowed for an almost unlimited number of variations, with the same general structure.

In those days, a .us domain name was cheaper than the gTLDs. Though the cost differed depending on which registrar a registrant selected, a .us domain name was generally less than $20 a year. Meanwhile, Network Solutions required a $100 sign-up charge and (starting in the third year) a $50 a year maintenance fee for gTLDs.[7]

Though the structure was logical and cheaper, provided for a large number of registrations, and was not confused with the existing TLDs, there were downsides of the domain that prohibited its growth.

It was difficult for possible registrants to know where to register a domain. Postel, the administrator, was responsible for the assignment of all .us names. Yet, as he noted in RFC 1480, "one person or even one group can't handle all this in the long run, so portions of the name space are delegated to others." In the case of .us, individuals and organizations could request an exclusive delegation to provide a registry and registrar services for a particular locality or localities. For example, someone with the requisite knowledge and infrastructure could request k12.tx.us to register all the kindergarten through twelfth-grade public schools in Texas or berkeley.ca.us for all sites located in Berkeley, California.

Under this structure, the .us registry had more than 8,000 subdomain delegations to more than 800 individuals and entities.[8] While this registration model allowed for commercial entities to provide name registration services, it also diversified the registration process, lessening the uniformity in both administrative practices (including fees) and the marketing of the larger domain.

Those registrants who managed to get through to their local registrars had fewer actual domain name options than those who registered under gTLDs. The early multilevel .us addresses were long, and because they were based on political geography, there were few catchy names. The ease of typing "www.amazon.com," for example, would have been replaced by "www.amazon.seattle.wa.us." While for local businesses an address like "www.pizzaplace.dover.de.us" could actually benefit business, for companies aiming for a national audience, the structure was less than ideal.

In addition, though the system was based on an easily recognizable structure, its use created confusion among many of the novice Internet users who continued to join the online community. With little education about the availability and structure of .us sites and the overwhelming attention that was given to .com sites, the throngs of relatively new Internet users found the .us sites confusing. Though many schools opted for .k12.state.us addresses, others chose to place their sites within the .org and .com name spaces.[9] Similarly, less than half the nation's cities used .us as their official name space and often opted for .org and .com addresses.[10]

Despite the relative popularity of .us addresses among state governments, libraries, and schools, throughout the 1990s, .us domain names had not proved particularly popular among individuals and businesses. "A lot of people just don't know it exists," Jon Postel told a *Wired News* reporter in 1997. "Then there's the length of the addresses—people don't like it."[11] While the lack of recognition and long .us addresses were bars to registration, so too was its attention-seeking companion, .com.

As an abbreviation for "commercial enterprises," the gTLD .com subconsciously represents not only the staggering economy in the 1990s but also the nation's free-market cultural foundations. The American culture is rooted in the quest to attain the American dream, an American social ideal that stresses egalitarianism and especially material prosperity.[12] The use and popularity of .com is a technological manifestation of that reality. It is therefore of little surprise that with more than 21 million registrations, .com has been the most popular domain ending.[13]

On July 1, 1997, as part of the Clinton administration's "Framework for Global Electronic Commerce," the president directed the secretary of com-

merce to privatize, increase competition in, and promote international participation in the Domain Name System.[14] In response to the directive,
amidst pressure for new gTLDs and to reduce conflicts between American
companies and others vying for the same .com domain name, many began
to see .us as an alternative to the gTLDs. In 1998, the United States National Telecommunications and Information Administration (NTIA), a
Commerce Department agency, published a notice that briefly addressed
the governance of .us. "Some in the Internet community have suggested that
the pressure for unique identifiers in the .com gTLD could be relieved if
commercial use of the .us space was encouraged. Commercial users and
trademark holders, however, find the current locality-based system too
cumbersome and complicated for commercial use."[15] Though it would take
several years, this notice signaled the shift in American priorities from the
virtual abandonment to the commercial exploitation of the .us name space.

Public comments to the notice continued the dialogue. Though there was
disagreement as to exactly how the process should continue, most of those
who commented supported an evolution of the .us domain to make the
name space more attractive to commercial users.[16]

Meanwhile, Postel continued to spread the word that, because of increased operating costs, it might be necessary for ISI to begin charging .us
locality name registrars; this likely would have filtered down to increase the
cost of registering .us domain names. "It turns out that we have avoided
that by obtaining further funding through 30-Sep-98," Postel wrote in an
e-mail in June 1998.[17] "ISI will need some funds from a new source to continue management of the US domain after 30-Sep-98."[18] As part of that effort, Postel had some meetings with the United States Postal Service (USPS),
one of the few groups to take an interest in the domain. The USPS entered
the conversation as it aggressively tried to assume authority of .us. It proposed to provide the necessary funding for the IANA to continue operating
.us and would also work with the IANA to make the transition to the USPS.

The desire on the part of the USPS was clear. Though stamp prices were
increasing, the use of e-mail was rising, and phone call prices were going
down. Technology was having a negative financial impact on the Postal Service; instead of beating its competitors, the USPS sought to join them.

According to the September 11, 1998, USPS discussion draft that was
sent to Postel, both a structure and a policy had been drafted. The USPS
saw .us as a national asset that should be used by both individuals and
businesses; it also believed that the U.S. government should act as coordi-
nator of, and set policies for, .us. "Its authority should not be given to the
private sector." Later, history would show that the U.S. government dis-
agreed with this assessment.

In the draft, the USPS identified that creating organizational partitions, limiting spam, ensuring privacy, and encouraging private sector involvement would be major challenges to its administrating the domain. While it then sought to respond to each of the challenges, resolving to "do all that is legally permissible to mitigate the problems associated with spamming" was hardly a concrete enough policy to implement. The USPS later formalized its position in a comment to the NTIA.[19]

The public's perception that the USPS was poorly organized worked to the disadvantage of the proposal.[20] In August 1999, the proposal had been scheduled to go before the House Commerce Committee but was postponed. Critics of the proposal argued that the USPS had few technical capabilities and no relevant expertise in domain name administration.[21] Representative Christopher Cox was concerned that the USPS would "leverage their existing monopoly and the advantages they have—not paying taxes, not being regulated the same way—to disadvantage their competitors."[22] Other groups raised the concern that privatizing the administration would lessen the public service aspects of the domain. With waning interest from the Postal Service, the redelegation to the USPS did not occur.

Reinitiating the discussion to redelegate .us, in August 2000, the NTIA requested comments on a draft statement that was expected to be incorporated in a request for proposals for management and administration of the .us domain space. Responses were sent from individuals, associations, and corporate entities, each with a variety of concerns and possible solutions.[23]

Once again, that the domain would not be used for the benefit of the public was a growing concern. Envisioning the .us name space as not a twin of the gTLDs but as a unique sibling, many groups proposed using the space with the specific goal of advancing the public interest. The American Library Association, for example, wrote, "The Internet was created with public funds. Its original purpose was to serve scholarship, research, and education. . . . We believe that commercial interests will be well represented in the ICANN debates over expanding the gTLD space and that overcrowding of the .com TLD will be relieved soon. Thus, it would be a serious mistake to use .us to address that issue. As the Internet is privatized, the .us TLD is one of the few potential levers remaining by which government can protect and advance public purposes."[24] The Media Access Project worked to develop "a proposal to use the .us ccTLD to promote civic discourse, enhance opportunities for non-commercial speech at a local and national level, and raise funds to address the digital divide."[25]

The debate over the true meaning of "public interest" is probably as great as the dispute between public and private interests. Some philosophers argue that the expression "public interest" has been so diluted that it would be better to abandon it altogether.[26] Still, for years, in each of its forms,

public interest concerns have been a part of American communications policy.[27] The notion of working for the public interest has roots not only in
American social policy but also in ccTLD policy. According to RFC 1591,
designated managers of ccTLDs are trustees for the delegated domain and
have a duty to serve the community.[28] Meanwhile, control of the domain,
which had been under the auspices of ISI, devolved back to the Department
of Commerce in October 2000 pending the redelegation.[29]

Based on the comments, on June 13, 2001, the NTIA issued the notice of
intent to release a request for quotations for management and coordination
of the usTLD.[30] It noted that, while a considerable number of parties had
expressed a desire for the continued operation and support of the locality-
based usTLD structure, the multilevel structure limited the domain's commercial attractiveness. "It has been suggested that a more generic space
would greatly increase the utility of the usTLD. Therefore, this request for
proposals not only encompasses the existing functions of the usTLD but also
functions that will facilitate the registration of second-level domains directly
under the usTLD."[31]

The future of .us was taking shape. While it would incorporate the location
entrenched hierarchy, it would also allow for domains in the general .us space
as well. Like the United States itself, it would seek to accommodate differing
motivations and opinions regarding the governance of the .us name space. It
also would be required to have a Uniform Dispute Resolution Policy (UDRP),
an enhanced WHOIS directory, and a preregistration (sunrise) procedure to allow trademark owners to register their marks before they are released to the
general public.

After just over a month, on July 27, 2001, the NTIA closed the bidding
process. Many politicians, computer users, libraries, and other public interest groups soon expressed their concerns that a vital public resource would
be given away to a commercial business that might not have the public's
best interests at heart. They argued that the process should have been al-
lotted more time to allow for more thought.[32] Still, others argued that time
was of the essence to allow a new delegate to take control of the domain
that was, at that point, being overseen by a transitional administrator.

Throughout American history the speed of government has been debated—
it is either too fast or too slow:

A democratic government inevitably moves more slowly—and sometimes less
efficiently—than a government where power is concentrated in the hands of
one individual or a small group. But the American experience throughout history has been that hasty government action is often ill-considered and harm-
ful. If the price of full public debate on all major issues is a relative loss of efficiency, it is a fair price and one the American people willingly pay. Moreover,

in times of national emergency the government has proved it can move swiftly and effectively to defend the national interest.[33]

Only time will tell whether the move to redelegate .us was, in fact, timed appropriately.

NeuStar, Inc., a private Washington, D.C., company, was delegated .us and assumed operational responsibility for the relaunched .us in November 2001.[34] Under the new policies, registrants of .us domain names must be U.S. citizens or people who live in the United States, an entity that is organized under the laws of the United States, or a foreign entity that has a bona fide presence in the United States.[35] An appropriate registrant can register names directly under .us or in the locality-based system. Despite its attempts to appease each of the interest groups, several of NeuStar's policies have drawn criticism.

While many corporate trademarks were reserved for companies to register during a specified sunrise period, public interest advocates argued that the process to reserve names was arbitrary and not enough public interest terms were reserved. As a result, the public at large was able to register "democrats.us," "republicans.us," and "freespeech.us," for example. Others argued that the company's process was adequately open to consultation from the larger public interest community. NeuStar responded by noting that it was both impossible and inappropriate to reserve every possible term.[36]

Citing the importance of .us as a national public resource and the need to preserve and enhance the value of the .us Internet address to all users, NeuStar developed a Registration Review Policy.[37] Accordingly, NeuStar will review, for possible deletion, all registrations that contain any of the "Seven Filthy Words," which were the subject of the 1978 Supreme Court case *Federal Communications Commission v. Pacifica Foundation*.[38]

Many registrants who had used the prohibited words before the policy took effect in April 2002 have had their domains deleted and have since raised the irony that a domain registry bearing the initials of the United States, a purported haven of free speech, practices a form of censorship.[39] According to NeuStar's statement, the purpose of the restrictive language policy is to preserve and enhance the value of the .us name space for all users. As a result, many see the policy as an effort to protect children and the public and not to arbitrarily restrict speech.[40]

While Americans value their constitutional First Amendment right to prevent the passing of laws to abridge free speech, there are circumstances when some abridgment is legally and socially permissible. This is most true when it comes to protecting children.[41] To make the Internet, and the .us name space in particular, safer for children, when NeuStar was delegated

.us, it agreed to set up a second-level domain called .kids.us that would be restricted to material appropriate for children. While NeuStar developed plans to create a safe haven for children that was commercially viable, Congress also sought get involved.

In May 2002, the House of Representatives voted to bar chat rooms, instant messaging, and other interactive features from .kids.us unless NeuStar could certify that they were free of pedophiles and other online predators.[42] NeuStar responded that such restrictions would likely curb commercial development. Congress did not slow when NeuStar requested more time to put together the domain's policies. Instead, when it came time for the president to sign the legislation regarding .kids.us in December 2002, the Senate and NeuStar managed to work out a deal whereby if NeuStar will uphold its .kids.us obligations, it will receive an extra two years on its four-year contract to operate .us. According to the Dot Kids Implementation and Efficiency Act of 2002, in addition to prohibiting chatting and instant messaging, .kids.us websites are not allowed to link to sites outside the domain.[43] Senator John Ensign said, "The Dot Kids bill marks the fourth— and hopefully final—attempt by Congress to strike a careful balance between safeguarding children on the Internet while not infringing on First Amendment rights."[44]

The plan has its detractors. For example, Alan Davidson, the associate director of the Center for Democracy and Technology, argued that the policy sets a dangerous precedent for regulation of the domain name space because it "inappropriately involves the government in making decisions about what material should and should not be available on the Internet." [45] In addition, many have voiced concerns that the space will be ineffective in protecting children because their Internet use is not restricted to .kids.us sites.

In addition to crafting the .kids.us policies, NeuStar was also required to draft a dispute resolution policy for domain name conflicts in the .us name space. One of the reasons for the early hierarchical layering of .us was to allow for many names and prevent disputes over names. The opening of the domain's second level opened the door to a flood of possible cybersquatting (the act of registering another's trademark in bad faith) for commercial gain.

There are currently two dispute resolution providers for .us domain name complaints. The first, the American Arbitration Association, has had few cases to decide. The second, the National Arbitration Forum, has transferred twenty-three domains, denied three claims, and had one split decision as of the writing of this chapter.[46] The arbitrators apply NeuStar's dispute resolution policies, which have been criticized for being overly lenient toward trademark holders.

While NeuStar modeled the usDRP on the larger UDRP, its changes do manage to benefit trademark holders. For example, NeuStar's deletion of eleven words from its definition of "bad faith" could have a negative impact for those who are charged with cybersquatting. Section 4(b)(ii) of the UDRP's definition says, "[The following] shall be evidence of the registration and use of a domain name in bad faith. . . . You have registered the domain name in order to prevent the owner of the trademark or service mark from reflecting the mark in a corresponding domain name, provided that you have engaged in a pattern of such conduct."[47] NeuStar's policy deleted the final clause, "provided that you have engaged in a pattern of such conduct."[48] As Professor Jon Weinberg noted, this language was originally included because, without it, a trademark holder would not need to prove any negative conduct other than the registration of the name. "Even the World Intellectual Property Organization (WIPO) and the UDRP drafters were unwilling to make respondents into such wide-open targets unless they were actual cybersquatters, who had registered a whole bunch of such names," Weinberg wrote. "NeuStar has no such compunctions."[49]

In addition, while under the UDRP the domain name had to be both registered and used in bad faith, NeuStar merely requires registration in bad faith or use in bad faith, not both.[50] Weinberg wrote, "That way, even if a domain name has never been used at all (and has never been offered for sale, which is commonly understood to qualify as 'use'), a panelist can still read the registrant's mind and divine that it was 'registered in bad faith,' and should properly be transferred."[51]

These two examples show a tendency on the part of .us to favor entities—trademark holders—in the registration of domain names. In 2002, law professor Peter Maggs wrote, "The privatization of '.us' is following the pattern of development of intellectual property in the United States in recent years—that of giving away the public domain free of charge to private interests."[52]

In its infancy, .us was eclipsed by .com; while businesses and trademark holders were not interested in occupying the layered name space, state governments, schools, and public libraries proliferated. Now, however, through .us's modified structure and governance, the domain resembles not only the public interests but also the commercial interests that occupy American life.

Notes

1. Jed Graham, "Dot-Us Name Gives Spark to Lagging Domain Field," *Investor's Business Daily*, May 22, 2002, A6.

2. "Bogus Domain Name Seller Settles FTC Charges," United States Federal Trade Commission, December 3, 2002, www.ftc.gov/opa/2002/12/tld3.htm [accessed March 18, 2003].

3. Jon Postel, "Domain Name System Structure and Delegation" (Network Working Group, Request for Comments No. 1591), March 1994, www.rfc-editor.org/rfc/rfc1591.txt [accessed March 13, 2003].

4. See "ISO 3166 Maintenance Agency (ISO 3166/MA)," International Organization for Standardization, www.iso.ch/iso/en/prods-services/iso3166ma/index.html [accessed May 21, 2003].

5. See "Root-Zone Whois Information," IANA, www.iana.org/cctld/cctld-whois.htm [accessed March 18, 2003].

6. In April 2003, the registration rules for .edu were relaxed to include postsecondary institutions that are institutionally accredited by agencies on the U.S. Department of Education's list of Nationally Recognized Accrediting Agencies. Community colleges are included on the list, as are accredited cosmetology programs, among others. See Anick Jesdanun, "Expansion of '.Edu' Domain Name Approved," Associated Press, February 12, 2003, www.siliconvalley.com/mld/siliconvalley/news/5158440.htm [accessed March 18, 2003], and "Eligibility for the .edu Domain," Educause, www.educause.edu/asp/faq/faq.asp?code=EDUELIGIBILITY [accessed March 18, 2003].

7. "Pledging Allegiance to .us," *Wired News*, July 8, 1997, www.wired.com/news/politics/0,1283,5025,00.html [accessed March 18, 2003].

8. "Management and Administration of the .us Domain Space," NTIA, August 17, 2000, www.ntia.doc.gov/ntiahome/domainname/usrfc2/dotusrfc2.htm [accessed March 18, 2003]; for a list of domains and delegates, see "Delegated Subdomains," www.nic.us/register/delegated_subdomains.txt [accessed March 18, 2003].

9. See, for example, the Yahoo! list of New York high schools at http://dir.yahoo.com/Education/K_12/Schools/High_Schools/By_Region/U_S__States/New_York/Complete_List [accessed March 18, 2003].

10. "Domain Names Need Standard Format," *American City & County*, June 2000, www.muniweb.com/Happenings/Writings-ACC-6-00.htm [accessed March 18, 2003].

11. See note 7.

12. See "American Dream," www.m-w.com [accessed March 18, 2003].

13. "Registrations," Caslon Analytics, February 2003, www.caslon.com.au/metricsguide1.htm [accessed March 18, 2003].

14. See "Memorandum for the Heads of Executive Departments and Agencies," White House Office of the Press Secretary, July 1, 1997, http://clinton3.nara.gov/WH/New/Commerce/directive.html [accessed March 18, 2003].

15. "A Proposal to Improve Technical Management of Internet Names and Addresses Discussion Draft," NTIA, January 30, 1998, www.ntia.doc.gov/ntiahome/domainname/dnsdrft.htm [accessed March 18, 2003].

16. "Management of Internet Names and Addresses," NTIA, June 5, 1998, www.ntia.doc.gov/ntiahome/domainname/6_5_98dns.htm [accessed March 18, 2003].

17. E-mail thread, "US Domain Future Developments," June 1998, www.apnic.net/mailing-lists/apnic-talk/archive/1998/06/msg00011.html [accessed March 18, 2003].

18. See note 14.

19. "Public Comments," NTIA, October 2, 1998, www.ntia.doc.gov/ntiahome/domainname/usrfc/comments/10-2-98.htm [accessed March 18, 2003].

20. "Going Postal over .us Domain" *Wired News*, August 5, 1999, 2, www.wired.com/news/politics/0,1283,21123,00.html [accessed March 18, 2003].

21. "Postal Service Gets Reprieve over '.us,'" CNET News, August 5, 1999, http://news.com.com/2100-1023-229486.html [accessed March 18, 2003].

22. "Post Office Barred from .us?" *Wired News*, August 5, 1999, www.wired.com/news/politics/0,1283,21106,00.html [accessed March 18, 2003].

23. "Public Comments," NTIA, August 17, 2000, www.ntia.doc.gov/ntiahome/domainname/usrfc2/comments.html [accessed March 18, 2003].

24. ".us domain comments," American Library Association, October 6, 2000, www.ala.org/oitp/gov/comments.html [accessed March 18, 2003].

25. "Issues: Internet Governance," Media Access Project, www.mediaaccess.org/programs/governance [accessed March 18, 2003].

26. Denis McQuail, *Media Performance: Mass Communication and the Public Interest* (London: Sage, 1992), 21.

27. For the application of public interest concerns toward mass media, see generally McQuail, *Media Performance*; see also Michael P. McCauley et al. (eds.), *Public Broadcasting and the Public Interest* (New York: M. E. Sharpe, 2003), and Milton L. Mueller, *Ruling the Root: Internet Governance and the Taming of Cyberspace* (Cambridge, Mass.: MIT Press, 2002), 144.

28. See note 3.

29. Thor Olavsrud, "ISI Gives Up Administration of .us," *InternetNews.com*, November 29, 2000, www.internetnews.com/dev-news/article.php/10_522381 [accessed March 18, 2003].

30. While perhaps technically correct, the reference to the .us name space as "usTLD" is confusing. It appears as though it is a hierarchical companion to "gTLD" and "ccTLD" instead of actually being a subset of "ccTLD." There are few references to other ccTLDs and gTLDs that use this notation style, but it has become increasingly prominent in relation to .us.

31. "Coordination and Management of .us Top Level Domain (USTLD)," NTIA, May 31, 2001, www.ntia.doc.gov/ntiahome/domainname/usrfp/cbd52501.txt [accessed May 21, 2003].

32. "U.S. Closes Bidding on '.us' Domain Bids," Reuters, July 27, 2001, www.thestandard.com/wire/0,2231,16785,00.html [accessed March 18, 2003].

33. Richard C. Schroeder and Nathan Glick, "Chapter 7, The Democratic Process," *An Outline of American Government*, 1989, http://usinfo.state.gov/usa/infousa/politics/govworks/oag-pt7.htm [accessed March 18, 2003].

34. "NTIA Announces Award to NeuStar to Manage .us Domain," NTIA press release, October 29, 2001, www.ntia.doc.gov/ntiahome/press/2001/us_102901.htm [accessed March 18, 2003].

35. See "The usTLD Nexus Requirements" .us, 2002, www.us/policies/docs/ustld_nexus_requirements.pdf [accessed March 18, 2003].

36. See David McGuire, "Consumer Groups Decry 'Dot-US' Policies," *Newsbytes*, April 29, 2002, www.washingtonpost.com/ac2/wp-dyn?pagename=article&node=&contentId=A2413-2002Apr29&notFound=true [accessed March 18, 2003].

37. "Registration Review Policy," .us, April 22, 2002, www.us/policies/docs/registration_review_policy.pdf [accessed March 18, 2003].

38. The words that will be reviewed according to NeuStar's policy are "shit," "piss," "fuck," "cunt," "cocksucker," "motherfucker," and "tits." In *Pacifica*, 438 U.S. 726, a Pacifica Foundation radio station broadcasted George Carlin's satiric monologue "Filthy Words," which listed and repeated a variety of colloquial uses of seven words you could not say on the public airwaves. A father who heard the broadcast while driving in the afternoon with his young son complained to the Federal Communications Commission (FCC). The case made its way up to the Supreme Court. It held that despite constitutional First Amendment free-speech concerns, the FCC had the authority to sanction the radio station for airing indecent materials in the afternoon. See *FCC v. Pacifica*, 438 U.S. 726, http://caselaw.lp.findlaw.com/scripts/getcase.pl?court=US&vol=438&invol=726 [accessed February 25, 2003].

39. See e-mail thread, ".US Registry Deleting Domain Names Retroactively!!" September 2002, http://lists.NeuStar.biz/pipermail/policy-forum/2002-Sept./000000.html [accessed March 18, 2003].

40. Despite the apparent desire to protect vulnerable people from such language, limiting the seven words fails to make the name space any more wholesome. For example, while "tits" was a forbidden word and tits.us is not registered, "titties.us," "boobs.us," and "boobies.us" have been registered. So, too, were such "dirty terms" as "cock.us," "ass.us," and "pussy.us." See the .us WHOIS database at www.whois.us [accessed March 18, 2003]; for the Registration Review Policy Announcement, April 23, 2002, see www.lextext.com/NeuStardirtywords.html [accessed March 18, 2003].

41. See, for example, *New York v. Ferber*, 458 U.S. 747, 757 (1982) ("Accordingly, we have sustained legislation aimed at protecting the physical and emotional well-being of youth even when the laws have operated in the sensitive area of constitutionally protected rights"), and *Paris Adult Theatre I v. Slaton*, 413 U.S. 49, 113 (1973) (arguing that "in the absence of distribution to juveniles, obscenity is constitutionally protected").

42. "Congress, NeuStar Clash over Kids' Zone," Reuters, September 13, 2002, http://zdnet.com.com/2100-1105-957878.html [accessed March 18, 2003].

43. See "Child-Friendly Second-Level Internet Domain," 47 USCS § 941 (2002), also at www.kids.us/content_policy/kids_efficiency_act.pdf [accessed March 18, 2003].

44. Roy Mark, ".Kids Legislation Heads to White House," InternetNews.com, November 18, 2002, www.isp-planet.com/news/2002/dot-kids_021118.html [accessed March 18, 2003]; for the latest news about .kids.us, see www.kids.us [accessed May 21, 2003].

45. Gretel Johnston, "Senate Toys with Kid-Safe Domain," IDG News Service, September 13, 2002, www.pcworld.com/news/article/0,aid,104915,00.asp [accessed March 18, 2003].

46. ".us Domain Name Dispute Proceedings and Decisions," National Arbitration Forum, www.arbitration-forum.com/domains/caseresults_test.asp?FullText=&SearchType=EXACT&CaseNo=&CaseName=&Domains=.us&CommenceDate=&DecisionDate=&Complainant=&Respondent=&Status=&RulesetID=&Sort=CaseNo [accessed March 18, 2003].

47. See "Uniform Dispute Resolution Policy," ICANN, August 26, 1999, www.icann.org/udrp/udrp-policy-24oct99.htm [accessed March 18, 2003].

48. "usTLD Dispute Resolution Policy," .us, February 21, 2002, www.us/policies/docs/usdrp.pdf [accessed March 18, 2003].

49. Jonathan Weinberg, ".US Goes to NeuStar," ICANNWatch.org, November 1, 2001, www.icannwatch.org/article.pl?sid=01/11/01/204125&mode=thread [accessed March 18, 2003].

50. Compare (a)(iii) UDRP at www.icann.org/udrp/udrp-policy-24oct99.htm [accessed March 18, 2003] and (a)(iii) usDRP at www.us/policies/docs/usdrp.pdf [accessed March 18, 2003].

51. See note 49.

52. Peter B. Maggs, "The '.us' Internet Domain," *American Journal of Comparative Law* 50, no. 297 (2002), http://home.law.uiuc.edu/~pmaggs/domainus.pdf [accessed March 18, 2003].

~

CHAPTER TWELVE

Australia's .AU: Australia's Second Gold Rush

Jenny Sinclair

When country code top-level domains (ccTLDs) were developed, few could foresee the Internet that was marked by vast commercialization and quick profits. Indeed, the enormous success of .com may have helped to curb both the demand and the practical use for .us.

Jenny Sinclair, a reporter for Melbourne's The Age *and the* Sydney Morning Herald, *explains how as awareness of domain names grew, so too did the prospects for their commercial use and possible exploitation. As a result, many ccTLDs, including Australia's .au, and their computer savvy caretakers were thrust into a world they neither anticipated nor welcomed.*

There is a gap in this chapter; it is a Robert Elz–shaped gap. It is a gap that exists in almost every one of the 100 articles this writer has written about the Australian Domain Name System since 1996. Robert Elz, who is known on the web mostly by his initials, "kre," connected Australia to the Internet by sending and receiving the first true e-mail messages. It was Elz who, at domain name pioneer Jon Postel's direction, was given leave to both create and manage the .au name space.

By rights, his should be a household name, certainly in the more than 40 percent of Australian households that had an Internet connection in 2002. Instead, he is little known outside the specialized field of domain naming. Now that .au has moved beyond its roots, coming under the control of a so-called industry self-regulatory body, Elz and his efforts have receded. In many ways, the story of .au's establishment and the rocky road it took from being a benevolent fiefdom to an accountable public service is the story of the Internet's own maturing both in Australia and globally.

Elz was not acting alone in June 1989, when he established the Internet connection from the University of Melbourne to one maintained by computer scientist Torben Nielsen at the University of Hawaii. He had volunteered—or been volunteered by a group of academics and university technical managers—for the job.

Elz was already running a network transferring mail and files to Australian universities, but the network desperately needed improving. The Australian Vice-Chancellors Committee (comprised of the heads of all Australian universities) and the Commonwealth Scientific and Industrial Research Organization sponsored the creation of a network called AARNET, which then spawned the Australian Internet. The work was kick started by a mere A$800,000 (U.S.$440,000) federal grant.

Australia does not have a tradition of corporate largesse to research bodies; the main source of funding is from the government. In a way, this gives the researchers a little more freedom to play in their ivory towers—and the Internet was probably the most useful side effect of research spending ever.

While all the universities were involved, it was Elz who had the technical ability and the motivation to establish and run the link. According to the man who first employed him, Emeritus Professor Peter Poole, Elz was a "brilliant" student of information technology and law.[1]

The .com.au name space, which hosts about 85 percent of Australian-registered domain names, was for years subject to policies that restricted the names of sites. Elz prohibited the use of generic and geographic terms; he also banned terms in domain names that could be considered offensive. The rules were steadfast unless you were lucky enough to strike a time when someone was filling in for Elz or you managed to get him to see your point of view. That was not always easy. Elz, a notoriously self-contained and incorruptible technician working from the computer department at the University of Melbourne, rarely explained his decisions and would reply only to e-mails he deemed worth the effort.

More seriously, by late 1996, the number of Australian businesses rushing to develop an Internet presence threatened to overwhelm Elz's physical ability to register names. Delays were mounting, and even among government-shy Australian entrepreneurs, questions were being asked about who this Elz character was anyway to be in charge of something as important as the Internet. His refusal to explain himself publicly only made the questions louder.

Only twice, via e-mail, has Elz ever responded to my inquiries; I am not alone. One of Australia's leading current affairs programs, *Four Corners*, once convinced Elz to participate in a web forum.[2] Even then, he did not appear on camera. Apart from these instances, Elz has maintained an aloofness toward the media for public forums and meetings.

His appearances on web forums, which are usually about high-level technical matters, are always to the point. I e-mailed him several times about this chapter, seeking comment and input. He chose not to reply. So, like me, you will have to make do with traces—with what others say, with his writings, and with the idea of someone who created something and did not want to give it up.

By late 1996, Elz had a backlog of thousands of .com.au names to process. As he said in the *Four Corners* forum, "People were starting to get desperate for .com.au registrations to get handled more quickly than I had been able to."[3]

Professor Peter Gerrand of the University of Melbourne then stepped in. Gerrand was personally familiar with Elz and was already head of domain name registrar Melbourne IT, which was set up to do research and commercially develop the university's intellectual property.[4] Gerrand brokered a deal with Elz that granted Melbourne IT the right to sell domain names within the .com.au name space. With the ability to sell .com.au domains, Melbourne IT's main activity became domain naming; the A$100 (U.S.$55) fee per name quickly became a river of cash. Their license to sell .com.au domains was technically nonexclusive, but effectively they had created a monopoly on the Australian domain naming market right at the start of the .com boom.

In December 1999, Melbourne IT floated its shares on the Australian stock exchange. Within a day, shares offered at A$2.20 (U.S.$1.20) leaped to A$9.10 (U.S.$5). At one point, Melbourne IT's market capitalization soared to more than A$100 million (U.S.$55 million). At its high, a share was valued at almost A$17 (U.S.$9); at its low after the .com crash, a share was valued at A$0.19 (U.S.$0.10).

The technical community, made up of Internet Service Providers, web hosts, developers, and even Melbourne IT's own name resellers, was already beginning to worry about how to democratize the naming system. From the outset, the Melbourne IT license was intended to be only an interim measure.

"Everyone was happy for about six months because the backlog got cleared; then everybody started to object like crazy because they realized they had given 90 percent of the domain name space to a monopoly organization," said Mark Hughes, who was a board member of an e-business body called TradeGate at the time.[5] Hughes later joined the board of auDA, which now runs the .com.au name space, and briefly served as its chief executive. He said, "Then there was this long attempt to set up what should have been set up first, i.e., a regulatory authority."

That was easier said than done. Members of technical groups like the Internet Society of Australia (ISOC-AU) and other early Internet libertarians soon lined up against those who saw .au as a chance to create new businesses.[6] Melbourne IT was often cast as the villain by the old-school, public service types.

The first attempt at creating an industry body to run .au was the Australian Domain Name Authority (ADNA), which was set up in June 1997.[7] According to Hughes, ADNA never stood a chance. "It had no authority and it had no money," Hughes said. Perhaps not surprisingly, Elz had an uncompromising attitude toward ADNA and its successors. According to Hughes, his position was, "If you show me you have the support of everybody, or the community, then I'm happy to transfer the authority."

When Elz was pressed as to what he would constitute as being support, he failed to answer. As a result, he created a hurdle that was impossible to define or measure. The fact that a number of groups showed their discontent for ADNA lessened its chances of making an impact. ISOC-AU, for example, objected that ADNA was too dominated by the registrars, such as Melbourne IT. "The Internet was changing from its original education and community focus, where a lot of input had come from entities like ISOC-AU, to where a lot of the noise was all about business," Hughes said.

Despite a vocal opposition, as the .com.au dollars flowed in, monopolistic Melbourne IT was becoming increasingly powerful. After nearly two years of stalled attempts at getting ADNA to work, its plans were shelved. A new body, auDA, was formed in April 1999.[8] It approached the task of creating a body that would take over the maintenance of the Australian domain space, with a very businesslike perspective. It recognized three types of voting members: demand class (people who buy names), supply class (people who sell names), and representative associations (groups like the Australian Internet Industry Association and ISOC-AU).

The inclusiveness of the group was always going to be a sticking point. Ever since the nineteenth century, when gold miners from around the world staged a bloody revolt against arbitrary policing and mining license fees, Australians have considered questioning authority and insisting on "having a say" to be their birthright, if not a duty.

At its inception, auDA was similar to ADNA; it had no money and no authority to make changes to the .au policies and procedures. In the meantime, the Australian government had become concerned. "The government did feel there was a need to ensure that the administration of .au was done in a way which was accountable to the full Internet community—that was increasingly becoming the full [Australian] community as a whole," said Dr. Paul Twomey, who was at that time the head of Australia's National Office of the Information Economy (NOIE).[9] Twomey was not only the Australian government's top bureaucrat on Internet issues but also, for a time, the chair of the powerful Governmental Advisory Committee of the Internet Corporation for Assigned Names and Numbers (ICANN). In March 2003, he was appointed ICANN's new president and chief executive officer.[10]

Hughes and the other auDA board members wanted government help but not too much of it. "The trick with any regulatory authority is to make sure the government is not going to move in and do it themselves," Hughes said. "The Government was saying very strongly 'We're not going to do it; you do it.'" While Hughes personally would have been happy for the government to step in, to get action, his view was not widely shared.

In fact, auDA had to beg the government for help. In a classic conundrum, auDA could not claim the right to manage .au until it showed it could both manage policy and run the system—which it could not do without funding for staff and advisers. Yet, without government assistance, the money needed for staff would have to come from the very organizations the body was seeking to control, particularly Melbourne IT.

Given that a key aim for auDA was to introduce competition between the .com.au registrars, monopoly registrar Melbourne IT was understandably reluctant to provide the necessary funding. Hughes said everyone took a hands-off approach to auDA yet still expected it to act. "We struggled along for about two years," Hughes said. "At the end of two years we made a board resolution which said 'This isn't going to work; we need government input.'"

In addition to asking the government for assistance, some auDA members came up with a secret and potentially divisive alternative plan; auDA had been given the rights to sell domain names within the .com.au name space, and Hughes said the plan was for the body to unilaterally appoint new registrars to force competition with Melbourne IT and to create a cash flow. On being told of the plan, the government's NOIE responded by granting a second staff member to help with policy development work; the group worked with the keen interest of Twomey, whose intervention Hughes credits with several breakthroughs.[11]

The most important outcome was the signing of a funding agreement between Melbourne IT and auDA. In late 1999, after much discussion, Elz was convinced to redelegate the authority he had in .com.au to auDA.[12] The transfer allowed auDA to sign a funding agreement with the reluctant Melbourne IT.

With some .com dollars flowing its way, auDA could finally turn its attention to the actual naming system rather than the tortuous world of Internet politics. In January 2000, it appointed its first chief executive, a veteran former civil liberties campaigner, Joseph O'Reilly. Despite a history of working well in highly politicized organizations, O'Reilly found the boisterous Australian Internet community to be too much; he resigned after less than a month on the job. Hughes took over as acting chief executive officer, and auDA soldiered on.

In October 2000, Chris Disspain agreed to run auDA. Disspain, a British-trained corporate lawyer who had already been the chairman of one .com company, joined an organization that he says had "no staff and had never really had any staff" and a board that was "used to making decisions that would normally be made by an executive."[13]

With only a couple of weeks to get a business and policy plan together before the annual general meeting, auDA had no office; Disspain was working from home. His primary concern, however, was the dispersed ownership of the .au domain's various elements. Despite having the authority to manage .com.au registrations, auDA did not own auNIC, the main Australian database of names. Despite the apparent need for full control, he said there was no plan for getting control of .au when he arrived.

Meanwhile, two panels were requesting comments on how to introduce new naming policies and the all-important competition in name sales. Regardless of the panels' efforts, Disspain knew that there was no prospect of being able to implement their findings without auDA having control over .au.

In December 2000, Senator Richard Alston, Minister for Communications, Information Technology, and the Arts, formally endorsed auDA as being "an appropriate entity to manage the .au domain space."[14] At the same time, the Australian government had passed legislation reserving the right to redelegate .au to the Australian Communications Authority.[15]

"There was never any intention that we should take it over," Twomey said. It was a procedural matter and a backup, but it also may have helped focus the minds of a group that—to Twomey's sometime frustration—nursed grudges and political battles for years. As a bureaucrat, Twomey never could understand the aversion to government authority over the web. "The philosophy was that we needed a representative body to administer it in the broad public interest," Twomey said.

To administer .au, Disspain also needed to secure either delegation or agreement on delegation from holders of the ten other second-level domains, like .edu.au (for education) and .id.au (for associations). Several of the secondary name space delegates signed funding and licensing agreements but did not actually hand over their delegation powers until the actual effective date of the new system. Elz himself was still managing .org.au, with significant delays, as well as .id.au, which was by now moribund.

Disspain said he was told time after time that auDA could not get full control of .au without Elz's agreement. Members of the board told him, the Domain Name System e-mail list for Australian domain naming told him, people at ICANN told him, and Melbourne IT told him; even Elz himself insisted that the handover of the authority over these domains had to be by agreement.

Elz, for all his eccentricities, was and is highly respected for the work he had done for .au. No one wanted to appear to be dumping on the guy who had set up and maintained the integrity of the system for so long.

Yet, when at a meeting Elz told Disspain, "I'm not satisfied that the community believes auDA is the right body [to run .au]," Disspain finally gave up on Elz. He then questioned all those who told him he needed Elz to agree. After all, he thought, the board was elected from the wider industry. It had support from ISOC-AU and the Australian Internet Industry Association, which meant that everyone from the techies to the suits was willing to work with the body.

Elz told Disspain that he meant the whole community—even people who did not use the web. "That's fine," Disspain replied. "Even the Australian Government supports us; and the only the body that represents the community at that level is the government."

While Elz still refused to agree, Disspain tried a new tactic. He would let others pursue Elz's agreement, and he would play bad cop. Disspain decided to formally ask the Internet Authority for Assigned Names and Numbers (IANA) to redelegate .au to auDA. "It was the only way to show that it was in the community's best interests," Disspain said. It was a big step; to get anywhere in the redelegation process through IANA, auDA had to allege that Elz was no longer doing the job correctly.

Disspain used .org.au as evidence that .au was not being managed consistently and effectively. There were a few other problems, not the least of which was the fact that a single computer that sat near Elz's desk at the University of Melbourne stored the only copy of the all-important root zone file—the list of all of the Australian domains and their related numerical IP address equivalents.

Disspain campaigned by asking the Australian government to write to ICANN to support him; he even wrote to Elz himself. Disspain was not worried about Elz having commercial or self-aggrandizing aims. He knew Elz's motives were pure but did not know was how far he was prepared to go. Would he, for instance, hide the zone files offshore? "I didn't have nightmares about it," Disspain said. "But I did wonder; is it ever going to end?"

It all came together in August 2001. IANA received a letter from Senator Alston that gave the government's strong support to auDA.[16] That letter joined another, received earlier that month, from the then chief executive of Melbourne IT, Adrian Kloeden.

Kloeden's letter urged IANA not to hand .au to auDA. He questioned auDA's ability to keep the system technically stable; he cast doubt on auDA's policy plans and said the body's integrity would be compromised if the handover of .au was other than voluntary on Elz's part. He wrote, "Melbourne IT . . . is not afraid of competition [in .au]," which is a claim that every other observer and participant would surely dispute since the company's millions were essentially founded on its ability to leverage its monopoly.[17] In a statement to IANA, Elz too objected. IANA's report on the deliberations noted, "Mr. Elz, however, has expressed concern that auDA is not fully formed and that, in practice, its base of participants is not as broad as desirable."[18] Both Kloeden and Elz suggested that if Elz could not run .au, the Australian government should do it. Yet, on August 31, 2001, IANA ruled that, in fact, auDA was "the appropriate delegee of the .au ccTLD."[19]

There was a price to pay for Australia. Disspain says that one condition of the transfer to auDA was that Australia was required to sign a country code registrar sponsorship agreement with ICANN, thereby committing it to provide funding for ICANN.[20] Australia was the first country to sign such an agreement; several other nations have since followed suit.[21]

Disspain said that the original system Elz set up had its strengths and that, while Elz never did explain to him why it was set up the way it was, it was something he could work with. The heavily debated naming restrictions, especially those on .com.au, have been credited with giving Australian Internet business some credibility. Until July 2002, only companies with a registered company or business name could have a .com.au web address.

An open slather registration system would have been harder to manage. "It's almost impossible to go backwards," Disspain said. "If it was open, you couldn't have closed it. I think it's an excellent system."

On July 1, 2002, auDA's reforms finally took effect; seven new registrars were appointed. Ending Melbourne IT's monopoly, the .id.au space was reopened to a rush of enthusiastic registrations by Australians wanting their personal space on the web, and new naming policies allowed companies to buy site names for products and promotions. Hundreds of new names with generic meanings were snapped up, and a system of regional place names to act as local portals began to be developed.

In the first six months of the new system, the total number of .au domain names registered grew by more than 10 percent, and the personal name space .id.au was adopted by 1,700 web-savvy Australians.

For the island of Australia, the Internet has helped overcome what is known as the tyranny of distance. Online, location was far less important, and the companies that saw that fact early—like naming firm Melbourne IT—knew that Australian know-how could compete almost equally in this new medium. Policymaker Twomey described the Australian government's eagerness to have him play a role in the global Domain Naming System in

1998: "We don't want the Internet to fail, it's too important for that." To Australia, naming was always a linchpin of a new way of dealing with the world. Twomey added, "Australians need to understand they've got to get there and be seen."[22]

In response to the demand for names, to the delight of the more reputable registrars, questionable sales practices by some domain name resellers have been curbed by an empowered auDA with the help of new contracts and Australia's competition authority. For the first time, there is a formal dispute resolution system for names wanted by more than one person. Interestingly enough, no such disputes had been litigated in all of Elz's management, which Disspain credits to the tight rules Elz created.

Hughes, the founder of auDA, like everyone who has dealt with Elz directly, goes to great pains to point out his integrity while at the same time saying that he held onto .au for far too long. "A lot of people have a lot of respect for Robert, for the way he has done the job, and for a decade without asking for any money," Hughes said. Twomey added, "I think if you build something up and it's been yours for a long period of time, it is hard to let go. People are human."

Since Elz lost .au and the subdomains, he has refrained from taking part in the wider public scene. While he continues to work at the University of Melbourne, his real contribution to the Internet remains financially uncompensated. As he said in the *Four Corners* forum, "There seems to be a lack of understanding that this is a hobby to me, not part of my job."

Now, years later, running the .au domains is neither Robert Elz's hobby nor his job. What remains of his work is a naming system that will affect the lives of all Australians.

Notes

1. "The Network Anniversary," *The Age* (Melbourne), June 22, 1999, Computers section, 1, also at www.peterpoole.info/files/ping.html [accessed March 18, 2003].

2. Australian Broadcasting Corporation: *Four Corners* Archives, transcript of "Domain Game," June 5, 2000, www.abc.net.au/4corners/stories/s136215.htm [accessed February 15, 2003].

3. See note 2.

4. Melbourne IT at www.melbourneit.com.au [accessed February 15, 2003].

5. Mark Hughes, telephone and e-mail interview by author, July 2002.

6. Internet Society of Australia at www.isoc-au.org.au [accessed February 15, 2003].

7. Home page of the now defunct Australian Domain Name Administration at www.auda.org.au/archive/adna [accessed February 15, 2003].

8. auDA home page at www.auda.org.au [accessed February 15, 2003].

9. Paul Twomey, telephone interview by author, July 2002; see also Australian National Office for the Information Economy at www.noie.gov.au [accessed February 15, 2003].

10. "ICANN Announces Dr. Paul Twomey as New President/CEO," ICANN, March 19, 2003, www.icann.org/announcements/announcement-19mar03.htm [accessed March 19, 2003].

11. NOIE, "Reforming .au Domain Name Administration," www.noie.gov.au/projects/information_economy/domains_au/index.htm [accessed February 15, 2003].

12. Robert Elz, "com.au Letter of Authority," November 15, 1999, www.auda.org.au/docs/letter-com.au.html [accessed February 15, 2003].

13. Chris Disspain, in-person interview by author, Melbourne, Australia, July 23, 2002.

14. Richard Alston, "Letter from Senator Richard Alston to Greg Watson (auDA)," December 31, 2000, www.iana.org/cctld/au/alston-to-watson-31dec00.htm [accessed February 15, 2003].

15. Australian Telecommunications Act of 1997, "Section 474: Declared Manager of Electronic Addressing," www.austlii.edu.au/au/legis/cth/num_act/ta1997214/s474.html [accessed February 15, 2003].

16. Richard Alston, "Letter from Senator Richard Alston to Stuart Lynn," July 4, 2001, www.iana.org/cctld/au/alston-to-lynn-04jul01.htm [accessed February 15, 2003].

17. Adrian Kloeden, "Message from Adrian Kloeden (Melbourne IT) to the IANA," August 3, 2001, www.iana.org/cctld/au/kloeden-to-lynn-03aug01.htm [accessed February 15, 2003].

18. IANA, "IANA Report on Request for Redelegation of the .au Top-Level Domain," August 31, 2001, www.iana.org/reports/au-report-31aug01.htm [accessed February 15, 2003].

19. See note 18.

20. For the agreement, see ".au ccTLD Sponsorship Agreement," ICANN, signed October 25, 2001, www.icann.org/cctlds/au [accessed February 15, 2003]. For the redelegation approval, see "Second IANA Report on Request for Re-Delegation of the .au Top-Level Domain," IANA, November 19, 2001, at www.iana.org/reports/au-report-19nov01.htm [accessed February 15, 2003].

21. See "ccTLD Resource Material," ICANN, www.icann.org/cctlds [accessed March 13, 2003].

22. Jenny Sinclair, "Net Warrior on a Mission," *The Age* (Melbourne), August 4, 1998, Computers section, 1.

CONCLUSION

~

Only Time Will Tell

Erica Schlesinger Wass

Every chapter in this book could have ended with the phrase, "Only time will tell." As quickly as technology develops, so too do the stories of country code top-level domains (ccTLDs). Often, with little or no fanfare, registration policies evolve and codes are delegated and, sometimes, redelegated. It is only conjecture whether and how the developments will work to achieve national visions and priorities.

This book examines the cultural links to, and history of, only 11 of the 243 codes that exist at the time of the writing. They were selected to provide an introduction not only to the individual codes but also to the processes, politics, and trends involved in the ccTLD system. There are many more stories to uncover and cultural connections to make. The framework for learning about the codes is multidimensional; it draws on the intersection between technology, politics, and local cultures.

There are four main areas where a nation's history and culture have affected the development of the name space. The first is in the historical acceptance of the code. Answering the question, When was the ccTLD first introduced and first used? shows not only where the code lies in comparison with its peers but also at what point the nation joined the larger global Internet community and the .com era overall.

The second indicator comes in the decisions regarding the structure of the name space. The specific question to ask is, Are registrants allowed to register directly under the ccTLD, or are they required to register under a number of second-, third-, or fourth-level domains?

The decision of whether to create a highly layered, hierarchical, or flat name space is not a quick decision; various codes have responded quite differently to the task. The early decisions were based on a combination of cultural and Internet-standard norms. Country code domain name administrators fell into two major camps: those who aspired to the diversity and popularity of .com and those who under a nationalistic ideal wanted to preserve the integrity of the name space. The former most often allowed registrants to register directly under their ccTLD, while the latter, those who sought to make sure that their name spaces reflected a hallmark of seriousness, chose a more layered structure.

The third indicator, the largest in scope, is the rule-making process. There are many questions to ask when examining a ccTLD's rules: Is the domain open, registerable by anyone, or closed, reserved to those with a presence in the host nation? Is the registration system one of prior assessment where registrants are required to submit supporting documents proving they are entitled to the domain, or can one register a domain quickly without such paperwork? How much does it cost to register a domain? Is the cost prohibitive for use by the local population, or is it low enough to encourage local use? Can individuals register domains, or is the process open only to organizations? Are there guidelines as to what domains can be registered within the names? Are some words forbidden? Is there a dispute resolution policy, and if so, whom does it favor?

While the rules put into place initially are useful to determine early interests and norms, it is their development over time that is truly illustrative of the interplay between larger cultural priorities and the name space. Therefore, changes in the policies must be closely examined; the often complicated reform processes are not made casually, but for a reason. It is the reason that motivates the change.

The fourth indicator is demonstrated by the nature of the content located in the code's name space and the popularity of the name space among the people. Questions to ask, when viewing sites in the name space and examining registration statistics are, Is the society in question generally seen as restrictive or open? Keeping the answer in mind, what types of content are hosted in the name space, and conversely, what is missing? Based on that information, is the name space popular? If so, with whom, and how does this reflect the economic and social priorities of the host nation? It is the why or the why not of each of these types of questions that shows how the policies and use of the domains reflect cultural norms.

News about ccTLDs has slowly been entering the mainstream media. For example, in New Zealand, the indigenous population has been granted its own piece of the national code with the creation of the .maori.nz name space.[1] In addition, as the nation of Afghanistan rebuilds in the physical world, it also constructed its virtual home. The Associated Press reported that, in a joint collaboration between the United Nations Development Program and the Afghan Ministry of Communications, .af, Afghanistan's ccTLD has been relaunched after several years of nonuse. The communications minister noted, "For Afghanistan, this is like reclaiming part of our sovereignty."[2]

Indeed, over the course of the ccTLDs' existence, the codes themselves have taken on a meaning that is distinct from their natural use. The idea that the codes somehow represent a nation's sovereignty and should therefore be under governmental control has continued to gain support. Will nations gain an increasing stake in the codes? Will the often disenfranchised find a virtual home in the national space more quickly than they have in the physical world? Will the codes even continue to be governed in their present form? Only time will tell.

Notes

1. See Gillian Bradford, ".maori.nz—A First for Indigenous People," *The World Today*, Australian Broadcasting Corporation, September 12, 2002, www.abc.net.au/worldtoday/s674648.htm [accessed March 19, 2003].

2. Todd Pitman, "Afghanistan to Launch Internet Domain," Associated Press, March 9, 2003, stacks.msnbc.com/news/882929.asp?cp1=1 [accessed March 19, 2003].

APPENDIX

~

Top-Level Domains

Generic Top-Level Domains (gTLDs)

Unrestricted (but intended for commercial registrants) .com
United States educational institutions .edu
United States government .gov
Organizations established by international treaties between governments .int
United States military .mil
Unrestricted (but intended for network providers, etc.) .net
Unrestricted (but intended for organizations that do not fit elsewhere) .org
Businesses .biz
Unrestricted use .info
For registration by individuals .name
Accountants, lawyers, physicians, and other professionals .pro
Air-transport industry .aero
Cooperatives .coop
Museums .museum

Country Code Top-Level Domains (ccTLDs)

Afghanistan .af
Albania .al
Algeria .dz
American Samoa .as

Andorra .ad
Angola .ao
Anguilla .ai
Antarctica .aq
Antigua and Barbuda .ag
Argentina .ar
Armenia .am
Aruba .aw
Ascension Island .ac
Australia .au
Austria .at
Azerbaijan .az
Bahamas .bs
Bahrain .bh
Bangladesh .bd
Barbados .bb
Belarus .by
Belgium .be
Belize .bz
Benin .bj
Bermuda .bm
Bhutan .bt
Bolivia .bo
Bosnia and Herzegovina .ba
Botswana .bw
Bouvet Island .bv
Brazil .br
British Indian Ocean Territory .io
Brunei .bn
Bulgaria .bg
Burkina Faso .bf
Burundi .bi
Cambodia .kh
Cameroon .cm
Canada .ca
Cape Verde .cv
Cayman Islands .ky
Central African Republic .cf
Chad .td
Channel Islands, Guernsey .gg
Channel Islands, Jersey .je
Chile .cl
China .cn

Christmas Island .cx
Cocos (Keeling) Islands .cc
Colombia .co
Comoros .km
Congo .cg
Cook Islands .ck
Costa Rica .cr
Côte d'Ivoire .ci
Croatia .hr
Cuba .cu
Cyprus .cy
Czech Republic .cz
Democratic People's Republic of Korea .kp
Democratic Republic of Congo .cd
Denmark .dk
Djibouti .dj
Dominica .dm
Dominican Republic .do
East Timor .tp
Ecuador .ec
Egypt .eg
El Salvador .sv
Equatorial Guinea .gq
Eritrea .er
Estonia .ee
Ethiopia .et
Falkland Islands .fk
Faroe Islands .fo
Fiji .fj
Finland .fi
France .fr
French Guiana .gf
French Polynesia .pf
French Southern Territories .tf
Gabon .ga
Gambia .gm
Georgia .ge
Germany .de
Ghana .gh
Gibraltar .gi
Greece .gr
Greenland .gl
Grenada .gd

Guadeloupe .gp
Guam .gu
Guatemala .gt
Guinea .gn
Guinea-Bissau .gw
Guyana .gy
Haiti .ht
Heard and McDonald Islands .hm
Honduras .hn
Hong Kong .hk
Hungary .hu
Iceland .is
India .in
Indonesia .id
Iran .ir
Iraq .iq
Ireland .ie
Isle of Man .im
Israel .il
Italy .it
Jamaica .jm
Japan .jp
Jordan .jo
Kazakhstan .kz
Kenya .ke
Kiribati .ki
Kuwait .kw
Kyrgyzstan .kg
Laos .la
Latvia .lv
Lebanon .lb
Lesotho .ls
Liberia .lr
Libyan Arab Jamahiriya .ly
Liechtenstein .li
Lithuania .lt
Luxembourg .lu
Macao .mo
Macedonia .mk
Madagascar .mg
Malawi .mw
Malaysia .my

Maldives .mv
Mali .ml
Malta .mt
Marshall Islands .mh
Martinique .mq
Mauritania .mr
Mauritius .mu
Mayotte .yt
Mexico .mx
Micronesia .fm
Moldova md
Monaco .mc
Mongolia .mn
Montserrat .ms
Morocco .ma
Mozambique .mz
Myanmar .mm
Namibia .na
Nauru .nr
Nepal .np
Netherlands .nl
Netherlands Antilles .an
New Caledonia .nc
New Zealand .nz
Nicaragua .ni
Niger .ne
Nigeria .ng
Niue .nu
Norfolk Island .nf
Northern Mariana Islands .mp
Norway .no
Oman .om
Pakistan .pk
Palau .pw
Panama .pa
Papua New Guinea .pg
Paraguay .py
Peru .pe
Philippines .ph
Pitcairn .pn
Poland .pl
Portugal .pt

Puerto Rico .pr
Qatar .qa
Republic of Korea .kr
Reunion .re
Romania .ro
Russia .ru
Rwanda .rw
Saint Kitts and Nevis .kn
Saint Lucia .lc
Saint Vincent and the Grenadines .vc
San Marino .sm
São Tomé and Principe .st
Saudi Arabia .sa
Senegal .sn
Seychelles .sc
Sierra Leone .sl
Singapore .sg
Slovakia .sk
Slovenia .si
Solomon Islands .sb
Somalia .so
South Africa .za
South Georgia and the South Sandwich Islands .gs
Spain .es
Sri Lanka .lk
St. Helena .sh
St. Pierre and Miquelon .pm
Sudan .sd
Suriname .sr
Svalbard and Jan Mayen Islands .sj
Swaziland .sz
Sweden .se
Switzerland .ch
Syria .sy
Taiwan .tw
Tajikistan .tj
Tanzania .tz
Thailand .th
Togo .tg
Tokelau .tk
Tonga .to
Trinidad and Tobago .tt

Tunisia .tn
Turkey .tr
Turkmenistan .tm
Turks and Caicos Islands .tc
Tuvalu .tv
Uganda .ug
Ukraine .ua
United Arab Emirates .ae
United Kingdom .uk
United States .us
United States Minor Outlying Islands .um
Uruguay .uy
Uzbekistan .uz
Vanuatu .vu
Vatican City State .va
Venezuela .ve
Vietnam .vn
Virgin Islands (British) .vg
Virgin Islands (U.S.) .vi
Wallis and Futuna Islands .wf
Western Sahara .eh
Western Samoa .ws
Yemen .ye
Yugoslavia .yu
Zambia .zm
Zimbabwe .zw

Source: "Top-Level Domains," ICANN, www.icann.org/tlds, and "Root-Zone Whois Information," IANA, www.iana.org/cctld/cctld-whois.htm [both accessed March 15, 2003].

Index

~

About the Contributors

Dana M. Gallup (dgallup@gallup-law.com) is a cofounder of, and initial investor in, the venture that licensed and marketed .md. A graduate of the University of Florida College of Law, he focuses his law practice in the area of labor and employment law.

Tushar A. Gandhi (tushar@mahatma.org.in) is the managing trustee of Mahatma Gandhi Foundation and the great-grandson of Mohandas K. Gandhi, the Mahatma. He has been closely connected with the Internet User's Community of India, a group that worked to introduce the Internet to India in the 1990s. He is working on the Mahatma on the World Wide Web Project of the Mahatma Gandhi Foundation (www.mahatma.org.in), which is the biggest multimedia electronic archive project in India and the most comprehensive website related to Mahatma Gandhi. In addition to actively promoting the use of the .in ccTLD, he works to extend the use and benefits of computers and the Internet to India's rural areas.

Toby E. Huff (Thuff@umassd.edu) is chancellor professor in the Department of Sociology and Anthropology at the University of Massachusetts, Dartmouth. He wrote *The Rise of Early Modern Science: Islam, China and the West* (1993), which has been translated into Arabic. A revised second edition with a new epilogue was released in mid-2003. He coedited, with Wolfgang

Schluchter, *Max Weber and Islam* (1999). In addition to his interests in the history of science (East and West), he continues his work on globalization and the Internet in the Asian and Muslim worlds.

Patrik Lindén (patrik.linden@iis.se) is a communications officer at the II Foundation (IIS), the organization responsible for the managing of .se and the development of Sweden's Internet infrastructure.

Martin Maguire (mmaguire@connect.ie) is the project director of Dublin ISP Connect-Ireland, and chief executive officer of Maguire, Mugen and Associates Ltd, a company specializing in developing solutions to nonprofits. This work is currently focused on the development of ambient technology–driven solutions to meet the needs of people with disabilities and the elderly. A graduate of Trinity College, Dublin, with a B.Sc. in public administration, he was responsible in 1987 for the first European Union community network and electronic database of community and political activities. In 1995 he set up Connect-Ireland, and in 1997 he established the .tp domain. He has since been approached by a number of people to discuss establishing country code domains.

Paiki Muswazi (paiki@uniswacc.uniswa.sz) is a special collections librarian at the University of Swaziland. He has an M.L.I.S. degree from the Simmons College Graduate School of Library and Information Science in Boston and is a member of the Special Libraries Association (SLA) and Swaziland Library Association (SWALA). Among other topics in library and information sciences, he has written extensively about the social implications of the Internet as it applies to developing countries like Swaziland.

Patricio Poblete (ppoblete@nic.cl) is administrative contact for NIC Chile, the domain name registry for the .cl country code top-level domain. Patricio has participated in the Internet Corporation for Assigned Names and Numbers (ICANN) as both a Domain Names Supporting Organization (DNSO) Names Council member and as a ccTLD Constituency Administration Committee (AdCom) member representing Latin America and the Caribbean. He is the director of the School of Engineering of the University of Chile and holds a Ph.D. in computer science from the University of Waterloo (Canada). He has been involved in the development of computer networks in Chile for the past eighteen years.

Jenny Sinclair (jsinclair@theage.com.au) has been a journalist for thirteen years and a technology reporter for Melbourne's *The Age* newspaper since 1996. Her articles also appear in the *Sydney Morning Herald*. She has a B.A.

in journalism from RMIT University and a bachelor of letters with a focus on cyberculture and hypertext studies from the University of Melbourne.

Richard StClair (stclair@niue.nu) is chairman of the Pacific Region Chapter of the Internet Society and serves on the board for the Asia Pacific Top Level Domain Forum (APTLD). He is the technical manager and cofounder of the Internet User's Society Niue and the holder of CET MCSE and CCIE certifications. He has a background in RF communications. Originally from San Jose, California, the entrepreneur retired in 1992 and ventured into communications development in emerging nations. Serving as a Peace Corps volunteer from 1994 to 1997, he was in the first group of Peace Corps volunteers to Niue and later moved back into private sector development. He lives on Niue with his Niuean wife, Sue.

Erica Schlesinger Wass (es231@columbia.edu) is a journalist and an attorney in New York City. A graduate of Barnard College, the Columbia University Graduate School of Journalism, and the Benjamin N. Cardozo School of Law, she writes about the Internet and the social implications of its use and governance. She is also a lecturer in the Strategic Communications Program at Columbia University and a frequent classroom guest lecturer on Internet law issues.

Peter K. Yu (peter_yu@msn.com) is assistant professor of law and director of the Intellectual Property and Communications Law Program at Michigan State University–DCL College of Law. He is also a research associate of the Programme in Comparative Media Law and Policy at the Centre for Socio-Legal Studies, University of Oxford. Born and raised in Hong Kong, he writes extensively and lectures frequently on intellectual property, international trade, communications law, international and comparative law, and the transition of legal systems in China and Hong Kong. He is the editor or coeditor of three books and is currently working on a casebook on international intellectual property law to be published by Carolina Academic Press.

www.ingramcontent.com/pod-product-compliance
Lightning Source LLC
Chambersburg PA
CBHW051239050326
40689CB00007B/998